THE
PSALTER
OF
KING DAVID

THE 1662 COVERDALE PSALTER
ARRANGED FOR ORTHODOX WORSHIP

ᛒ

BUKY PRESS

CONTENTS

Preface 8

Prayers 12

During Summer 21

During Winter 24

During Great Lent 27

The First Kathisma 34

The Second Kathisma 46

The Third Kathisma 60

The Fourth Kathisma 77

The Fifth Kathisma 93

The Sixth Kathisma 108

The Seventh Kathisma 127

The Eight Kathisma 144

The Ninth Kathisma 158

The Tenth Kathisma 173

The Eleventh Kathisma 189

The Twelfth Kathisma 209

The Thirteenth Kathisma 223

The Fourteenth Kathisma..238

The Fifteenth Kathisma...282

The Sixteenth Kathisma...267

The Seventeenth Kathisma..279

The Eighteenth Kathisma..297

The Nineteenth Kathisma..311

The Twentieth Kathisma..327

Acknowledgments...339

Copyright...340

7

PREFACE

PERHAPS the most enduring of all English versions of the book of Psalms is that of Myles Coverdale. Originally published in A.D. 1535 as part of one of the earliest English Bible translations, Coverdale's psalter grew in popularity such that it was adopted by the Church of England and printed in its Book of Common Prayer from the mid-16th century down to the present day.

Justly renowned for its majestic prose and poetic beauty, the Coverdale psalter even today holds a prominent place in public and private worship, not only within Anglicanism, but now in the Catholic and Orthodox churches also (especially via the Anglican Ordinariates and the Western Rites, respectively). While over time numerous revisions have been made in many countries, the psalter is herein presented in its quintessential 1662 form, with the following slight adjustments made to the text in order to best

8

prepare this publication for convenient use at prayer:

1. The holy name of God in Psalm 68 is transliterated in the 1662 psalter as JAH, but is here rendered as the Hebrew tetragrammaton יהוה in order to indicate that the sacred name should not be pronounced.

2. Subtitles (translated from the Septuagint) have been added to the psalms. The Latin incipits are retained, having become over the centuries an essential part of the Coverdale psalter.

3. Verse numbering has been omitted, and proper punctuation marks have been added mid-verse to the psalms, borrowing from the schemata found in *The Anglican Breviary* and the Oxford *Monastic Diurnal*. Here, asterisks replace the colons typically used to mark the half-verses in the English prayer-book tradition.

4. The psalter has been divided into kathismata and stases following the ancient Eastern tradition; therefore, the usual Anglican 30-day divisions have been omitted. In two instances (Psalm 116, and the seventeenth stanza of Psalm 119) where the difference between the Greek and Hebrew numbering would cause a psalm to be broken over two stases, the complete psalm has been placed after the stasis division.

Furthermore, Psalm 151 has been included for the sake of completeness. This psalm not having been among the manuscripts available to Coverdale, the version used here is a translation by the late Monk Joseph (Isaac Lambertsen) of Holy Trinity Orthodox Seminary.

In addition to these textual modifications, the usual beginning prayers and prayers following each stasis and kathisma have also been included; in certain places, a Maltese cross (✠) has been inserted to mark where the sign of the cross should be made.

Parts of this text are set in Bulgaria Moderna Pro. Please relate comments, concerns, or errors to the publisher at common_prayer@pm.me. Any issues raised will be rectified as quickly as practicable in order to help this book remain a worthy vehicle of prayer, as free as possible from distracting imperfections.

—M.B., December 2020

PRAYERS

OPENING PRAYERS...13
AFTER EACH STASIS 18
AFTER EACH KATHISMA.....................................19
DISMISSAL PRAYERS 20

OPENING PRAYERS

To be said when beginning prayers either in the morning, in the evening, or at any other time of the day.

O God, ✠ be merciful to me a sinner. *(Thrice.)*

If a priest leads the service:
Blessed ✠ is the Kingdom of the Father, and of the Son, and of the Holy Spirit: * both now and ever, and unto the ages of ages.
Amen.

Otherwise:
Through ✠ the prayers of our holy fathers, O Lord Jesus Christ, * have mercy on us and save us.
Amen.

The Trisagion Prayers

Glory ✠ to thee, O God, * glory to thee.

Throughout the year (omitted on the Saturday before Pentecost):
O Heavenly King, Comforter, Spirit of Truth, who art everywhere present and fillest all things, Treasury of good things and Giver of life: * Come and dwell in us, and cleanse us of all impurity, and save our souls, O Good One.

From the Resurrection of the Lord until the Feast of the Ascension:
Christ is risen from the dead, trampling down death by death, * and upon those in the tombs bestowing life. *(Thrice.)*

From Feast of the Ascension until its leavetaking:
Thou hast ascended in glory, Christ our God,
    granting joy to thy disciples by the promise of
    thy Holy Spirit. * Through thy blessing, they
    were assured that thou art the Son of God, the
    Redeemer of the world.
Holy ✠ God, Holy Mighty, Holy Immortal, *
    have mercy on us. *(Thrice.)*

Glory ✠ to the Father, and to the Son, and to the
    Holy Spirit, * both now and ever, and unto the
    ages of ages. Amen.

O Most Holy Trinity, have mercy on us. O Lord,
    blot out our sins. O Master, pardon our
    iniquities. * O Holy One, visit and heal our
    infirmities for thy name's sake.

Lord, have mercy. Lord, have mercy. * Lord, have
    mercy.

Glory ✠ to the Father and to the Son and to the
    Holy Spirit, * both now and ever, and unto the
    ages of ages. Amen.

Our Father, which art in heaven, hallowed be thy
  Name, thy kingdom come, thy will be done, in
  earth as it is in heaven. Give us this day our
  daily bread. And forgive us our trespasses, as
  we forgive them that trespass against us. And
  lead us not into temptation, * but deliver us
  from evil.

If a priest leads the service:
For thine is the kingdom, and the power, and the
  glory, of the Father, ✠ and of the Son, and of
  the Holy Spirit, * both now and ever, and unto
  the ages of ages.
Amen.

Otherwise:
O Lord Jesus Christ, Son of God, * have mercy on
  us and save us.
Amen.

Lord, have mercy. *(Twelve times.)*

Glory ✠ to the Father, and to the Son, and to the Holy Spirit, * both now and ever, and unto the ages of ages. Amen.

Come, ✠ let us worship our King and God. Come, ✠ let us worship Christ, our King and God. * Come, ✠ let us worship and bow before the only Lord Jesus Christ, the King and our God.

AFTER EACH STASIS

Glory ✠ to the Father, and to the Son, and to the
   Holy Spirit, * both now and ever, and unto the
   ages of ages. Amen.

Alleluia, alleluia, alleluia. * Glory to thee, O God.
   (Thrice.)

Lord, have mercy. Lord, have mercy. * Lord, have
   mercy.

Glory ✠ to the Father, and to the Son, and to the
   Holy Spirit, * both now and ever, and unto the
   ages of ages. Amen.

AFTER EACH KATHISMA

Glory ✠ to the Father, and to the Son, and to the Holy Spirit, * both now and ever, and unto the ages of ages. Amen.

Alleluia, alleluia, alleluia. * Glory to thee, O God. *(Twice.)*

Alleluia, alleluia, alleluia. * Glory to thee, O God, our hope. O Lord, glory be to thee.

DISMISSAL PRAYERS

It is truly meet to bless thee, the Theotokos, ever-
blessed and most blameless, and Mother of our
God. More honourable than the Cherubim, and
beyond compare more glorious than the
Seraphim, who without corruption gavest birth
to God the Word, * the very Theotokos, thee do
we magnify.

Glory ✠ to the Father, and to the Son, and to the
Holy Spirit, * both now and ever, and unto the
ages of ages. Amen.

Lord, have mercy. Lord, have mercy. * Lord, have
mercy.

Through ✠ the prayers of our holy fathers, O Lord
Jesus Christ, * have mercy on us and save us.
Amen.

DURING SUMMER

From the Sunday of Saint Thomas until the
Leavetaking of the Exaltation of the Holy Cross;
from the Forefeast of the Holy Nativity until the
Leavetaking of the Holy Theophany; and during
the weeks of Meatfare and Cheesefare.

MATINS..22
VESPERS..23

MATINS

The following kathismata are to be prayed at Matins throughout the summer.

SUNDAY .... II, III

MONDAY .... IV, V

TUESDAY .... VII, VIII

WEDNESDAY .... X, XI

THURSDAY .... XIII, XIV

FRIDAY .... XIX, XX

SATURDAY .... XVI, XVII

VESPERS

The following kathismata are to be prayed at Vespers throughout the summer.

MONDAY...VI

TUESDAY..XI

WEDNESDAY...XII

THURSDAY...XV

FRIDAY..XVIII

SATURDAY..I

DURING WINTER

From the Leavetaking of the Exaltation of the Holy Cross through the Sunday of the Prodigal Son.

MATINS...25

VESPERS..26

MATINS

The following kathismata are to be prayed at Matins throughout the winter.

SUNDAY..II, III, XVII

MONDAY..IV, V, VI

TUESDAY..VII, VIII, IX

WEDNESDAY..X, XI, XII

THURSDAY...XIII, XIV, XV

FRIDAY...XIX, XX

SATURDAY...XVI, XVII

VESPERS

The following kathismata are to be prayed at Vespers throughout the winter.

MONDAY XVIII

TUESDAY XVIII

WEDNESDAY XVIII

THURSDAY XVIII

FRIDAY XVIII

SATURDAY I

26

DURING GREAT LENT

MATINS...28
FIRST HOUR..29
THIRD HOUR.......................................30
SIXTH HOUR.......................................31
NINTH HOUR......................................32
VESPERS...33

MATINS

The following kathismata are to be prayed at
Matins throughout Lent.

SUNDAY ....II, III, XVII

MONDAY ....IV, V, VI

TUESDAY ....X, XI, XII

WEDNESDAY ....XIX, XX, I

THURSDAY ....VI, VII, VIII

FRIDAY ....XIII, XIV, XV

SATURDAY ....XVI, XVII

FIRST HOUR

The following kathismata are to be prayed at First
Hour throughout Lent.

TUESDAY XIII
WEDNESDAY II
THURSDAY IX

THIRD HOUR

The following kathismata are to be prayed at
Third Hour throughout Lent.

MONDAY..VII

TUESDAY...XIV

WEDNESDAY..III

THURSDAY..X

FRIDAY...XIX

SIXTH HOUR

The following kathismata are to be prayed at Sixth Hour throughout Lent.

MONDAY..VIII

TUESDAY..XV

WEDNESDAY..IV

THURSDAY...XI

FRIDAY...XX

NINTH HOUR

The following kathismata are to be prayed at
Ninth Hour throughout Lent.

MONDAY...IX
TUESDAY..XVI
WEDNESDAY..V
THURSDAY..XII

VESPERS

The following kathismata are to be prayed at Vespers throughout Lent.

MONDAY XVIII

TUESDAY XVIII

WEDNESDAY XVIII

THURSDAY XVIII

FRIDAY XVIII

SATURDAY I

THE FIRST KATHISMA

Psalm 1. *Beatus vir, qui non abiit.*

BLESSED is the man that hath not walked in the
counsel of the ungodly, nor stood in the way of
sinners, * and hath not sat in the seat of the
scornful.

But his delight is in the law of the Lord; * and in
his law will he exercise himself day and night.

And he shall be like a tree planted by the water-
side, * that will bring forth his fruit in due
season.

His leaf also shall not wither; * and look,
whatsoever he doeth, it shall prosper.

As for the ungodly, it is not so with them; * but
they are like the chaff, which the wind
scattereth away from the face of the earth.

Therefore the ungodly shall not be able to stand in
the judgement, * neither the sinners in the
congregation of the righteous.

But the Lord knoweth the way of the righteous; *
and the way of the ungodly shall perish.

Psalm 2. *Quare fremuerunt gentes?*

WHY do the heathen so furiously rage together? *
and why do the people imagine a vain thing?

The kings of the earth stand up, and the rulers take
counsel together * against the Lord, and against
his Anointed.

Let us break their bonds asunder, * and cast away
their cords from us.

He that dwelleth in heaven shall laugh them to
scorn: * the Lord shall have them in derision.

Then shall he speak unto them in his wrath, * and
vex them in his sore displeasure.

Yet have I set my King * upon my holy hill of
Sion.

I will preach the law, whereof the Lord hath said
unto me, * Thou art my Son, this day have I
begotten thee.

Desire of me, and I shall give thee the heathen for
thine inheritance, * and the utmost parts of the
earth for thy possession.

Thou shalt bruise them with a rod of iron, * and break them in pieces like a potter's vessel.

Be wise now therefore, O ye kings; * be learned, ye that are judges of the earth.

Serve the Lord in fear, * and rejoice unto him with reverence.

Kiss the Son, lest he be angry, and so ye perish from the right way; * if his wrath be kindled, (yea, but a little,) blessed are all they that put their trust in him.

Psalm 3. *Domine, quid multiplicati.*
A psalm of David. When he fled from the presence of his son Absalom.

LORD, how are they increased that trouble me! * many are they that rise against me.

Many one there be that say of my soul, * There is no help for him in his God.

But thou, O Lord, art my defender; * thou art my worship, and the lifter up of my head.

I did call upon the Lord with my voice, * and he heard me out of his holy hill.

I laid me down and slept, and rose up again; * for the Lord sustained me.

I will not be afraid for ten thousands of the
people, * that have set themselves against me
round about.

Up, Lord, and help me, O my God, * for thou
smitest all mine enemies upon the cheekbone;
thou hast broken the teeth of the ungodly.

Salvation belongeth unto the Lord; * and thy
blessing is upon thy people.

✠ SECOND STASIS ✠

Psalm 4. *Cum invocarem.*

For the end. A song of David among the Psalms.

HEAR me when I call, O God of my
righteousness: * thou hast set me at liberty
when I was in trouble; have mercy upon me,
and hearken unto my prayer.

O ye sons of men, how long will ye blaspheme
mine honour, * and have such pleasure in
vanity, and seek after leasing?

Know this also, that the Lord hath chosen to
himself the man that is godly; * when I call
upon the Lord, he will hear me.

Stand in awe, and sin not; * commune with your
   own heart, and in your chamber, and be still.
Offer the sacrifice of righteousness, * and put
   your trust in the Lord.
There be many that say, * Who will shew us any
   good?
Lord, lift thou up * the light of thy countenance
   upon us.
Thou hast put gladness in my heart, * since the
   time that their corn and wine and oil increased.
I will lay me down in peace, and take my rest; *
   for it is thou, Lord, only, that makest me dwell
   in safety.

Psalm 5. *Verba mea auribus.*
*For the end. A song of David concerning her that
inheriteth.*

PONDER my words, O Lord, * consider my
   meditation.
O hearken thou unto the voice of my calling, my
   King, and my God: * for unto thee will I make
   my prayer.

My voice shalt thou hear betimes, O Lord; * early
in the morning will I direct my prayer unto
thee, and will look up.

For thou art the God that hast no pleasure in
wickedness; * neither shall any evil dwell with
thee.

Such as be foolish shall not stand in thy sight; *
for thou hatest all them that work vanity.

Thou shalt destroy them that speak leasing: * the
Lord will abhor both the blood-thirsty and
deceitful man.

But as for me, I will come into thine house, even
upon the multitude of thy mercy; * and in thy
fear will I worship toward thy holy temple.

Lead me, O Lord, in thy righteousness, because of
mine enemies; * make thy way plain before my
face.

For there is no faithfulness in his mouth; * their
inward parts are very wickedness.

Their throat is an open sepulchre; * they flatter
with their tongue.

Destroy thou them, O God; let them perish
through their own imaginations; * cast them out

in the multitude of their ungodliness; for they have rebelled against thee.

And let all them that put their trust in thee rejoice: * they shall ever be giving of thanks, because thou defendest them; they that love thy Name shall be joyful in thee;

For thou, Lord, wilt give thy blessing unto the righteous; * and with thy favourable kindness wilt thou defend him as with a shield.

Psalm 6. *Domine, ne in furore.*
For the end. A psalm of David among the hymns for the eighth.

O LORD, rebuke me not in thine indignation, * neither chasten me in thy displeasure.

Have mercy upon me, O Lord, for I am weak; * O Lord, heal me, for my bones are vexed.

My soul also is sore troubled: * but, Lord, how long wilt thou punish me?

Turn thee, O Lord, and deliver my soul; * O save me for thy mercy's sake.

For in death no man remembereth thee; * and who will give thee thanks in the pit?

I am weary of my groaning; every night wash I my bed, * and water my couch with my tears.

My beauty is gone for very trouble, * and worn away because of all mine enemies.

Away from me, all ye that work vanity; * for the Lord hath heard the voice of my weeping.

The Lord hath heard my petition; * the Lord will receive my prayer.

All mine enemies shall be confounded, and sore vexed; * they shall be turned back, and put to shame suddenly.

✠ THIRD STASIS ✠

Psalm 7. *Domine, Deus meus.*
A psalm of David, which he sang to the Lord because of the words of Cush the Benjamite.

O LORD my God, in thee have I put my trust: * save me from all them that persecute me, and deliver me;

Lest he devour my soul, like a lion, and tear it in pieces, * while there is none to help.

O Lord my God, if I have done any such thing; *
   or if there be any wickedness in my hands;
If I have rewarded evil unto him that dealt friendly
   with me; * yea, I have delivered him that
   without any cause is mine enemy,
Then let mine enemy persecute my soul, and take
   me; * yea, let him tread my life down upon the
   earth, and lay mine honour in the dust.
Stand up, O Lord, in thy wrath, and lift up thyself,
   because of the indignation of mine enemies; *
   arise up for me in the judgement that thou hast
   commanded.
And so shall the congregation of the people come
   about thee: * for their sakes therefore lift up
   thyself again.
The Lord shall judge the people; give sentence
   with me, O Lord, * according to my
   righteousness, and according to the innocency
   that is in me.
O let the wickedness of the ungodly come to an
   end; * but guide thou the just.
For the righteous God * trieth the very hearts and
   reins.

My help cometh of God, * who preserveth them
  that are true of heart.
God is a righteous Judge, strong and patient; * and
  God is provoked every day.
If a man will not turn, he will whet his sword; * he
  hath bent his bow, and made it ready.
He hath prepared for him the instruments of
  death; * he ordaineth his arrows against the
  persecutors.
Behold, he travaileth with mischief; * he hath
  conceived sorrow, and brought forth
  ungodliness.
He hath graven and digged up a pit, * and is fallen
  on himself into the destruction that he made for
  other.
For his travail shall come upon his own head, *
  and his wickedness shall fall on his own pate.
I will give thanks unto the Lord, according to his
  righteousness; * and I will praise the Name of
  the Lord most High.

Psalm 8. *Domine, Dominus noster.*

For the end. A psalm of David concerning the winepresses.

O LORD our Governor, how excellent is thy Name
in all the world; * thou that hast set thy glory
above the heavens!

Out of the mouth of very babes and sucklings hast
thou ordained strength, because of thine
enemies, * that thou mightest still the enemy
and the avenger.

For I will consider thy heavens, even the works of
thy fingers; * the moon and the stars, which
thou hast ordained.

What is man, that thou art mindful of him? * and
the son of man, that thou visitest him?

Thou madest him lower than the angels, * to
crown him with glory and worship.

Thou makest him to have dominion of the works
of thy hands; * and thou hast put all things in
subjection under his feet;

All sheep and oxen; * yea, and the beasts of the
field;

The fowls of the air, and the fishes of the sea; *
and whatsoever walketh through the paths of
the seas.

O Lord our Governor, * how excellent is thy
Name in all the world!

THE SECOND KATHISMA

✠ FIRST STASIS ✠

Psalm 9. *Confitebor tibi.*

For the end. A psalm of David concerning the secrets of the Son.

I WILL give thanks unto thee, O Lord, with my whole heart; * I will speak of all thy marvellous works.

I will be glad and rejoice in thee; * yea, my songs will I make of thy Name, O thou most Highest.

While mine enemies are driven back, * they shall fall and perish at thy presence.

For thou hast maintained my right and my cause; * thou art set in the throne that judgest right.

Thou hast rebuked the heathen, and destroyed the ungodly; * thou hast put out their name for ever and ever.

O thou enemy, destructions are come to a perpetual end; * even as the cities which thou hast destroyed, their memorial is perished with them.

But the Lord shall endure for ever; * he hath also prepared his seat for judgement.

For he shall judge the world in righteousness, * and minister true judgement unto the people.

The Lord also will be a defence for the oppressed, * even a refuge in due time of trouble.

And they that know thy Name will put their trust in thee; * for thou, Lord, hast never failed them that seek thee.

O praise the Lord which dwelleth in Sion; * shew the people of his doings.

For when he maketh inquisition for blood, he remembereth them, * and forgetteth not the complaint of the poor.

Have mercy upon me, O Lord; consider the trouble which I suffer of them that hate me, * thou that liftest me up from the gates of death.

That I may shew all thy praises within the ports of the daughter of Sion: * I will rejoice in thy salvation.

The heathen are sunk down in the pit that they
made; * in the same net which they hid privily,
is their foot taken.

The Lord is known to execute judgement; * the
ungodly is trapped in the work of his own
hands.

The wicked shall be turned into hell, * and all the
people that forget God.

For the poor shall not alway be forgotten; * the
patient abiding of the meek shall not perish for
ever.

Up, Lord, and let not man have the upper hand; *
let the heathen be judged in thy sight.

Put them in fear, O Lord, * that the heathen may
know themselves to be but men.

Psalm 10. *Ut quid, Domine?*

WHY standest thou so far off, O Lord, * and hidest
thy face in the needful time of trouble?

The ungodly for his own lust doth persecute the
poor: * let them be taken in the crafty wiliness
that they have imagined.

For the ungodly hath made boast of his own
heart's desire, * and speaketh good of the
covetous, whom God abhorreth.

The ungodly is so proud, that he careth not for
God, * neither is God in all his thoughts.

His ways are alway grievous; * thy judgements
are far above out of his sight, and therefore
defieth he all his enemies.

For he hath said in his heart, Tush, I shall never be
cast down, * there shall no harm happen unto
me.

His mouth is full of cursing, deceit, and fraud; *
under his tongue is ungodliness and vanity.

He sitteth lurking in the thievish corners of the
streets, * and privily in his lurking dens doth he
murder the innocent; his eyes are set against the
poor.

For he lieth waiting secretly, even as a lion lurketh
he in his den, * that he may ravish the poor.

He doth ravish the poor, * when he getteth him
into his net.

He falleth down, and humbleth himself, * that the
congregation of the poor may fall into the hands
of his captains.

He hath said in his heart, Tush, God hath
forgotten; * he hideth away his face, and he will
never see it.

Arise, O Lord God, and lift up thine hand; * forget
not the poor.

Wherefore should the wicked blaspheme God, *
while he doth say in his heart, Tush, thou God
carest not for it.

Surely thou hast seen it; * for thou beholdest
ungodliness and wrong.

That thou mayest take the matter into thy hand, *
the poor committeth himself unto thee; for thou
art the helper of the friendless.

Break thou the power of the ungodly and
malicious; * take away his ungodliness, and
thou shalt find none.

The Lord is King for ever and ever, * and the
heathen are perished out of the land.

Lord, thou hast heard the desire of the poor; *
thou preparest their heart, and thine ear
hearkeneth thereto;

To help the fatherless and poor unto their right, *
that the man of the earth be no more exalted
against them.

Psalm 11. *In Domino confido.*
For the end. A psalm of David.

IN THE Lord put I my trust; * how say ye then to my soul, that she should flee as a bird unto the hill?

For lo, the ungodly bend their bow, and make ready their arrows within the quiver, * that they may privily shoot at them which are true of heart.

For the foundations will be cast down, * and what hath the righteous done?

The Lord is in his holy temple; * the Lord's seat is in heaven.

His eyes consider the poor, * and his eye-lids try the children of men.

The Lord alloweth the righteous: * but the ungodly, and him that delighteth in wickedness, doth his soul abhor.

Upon the ungodly he shall rain snares, fire and brimstone, storm and tempest; * this shall be their portion to drink.

For the righteous Lord loveth righteousness; * his countenance will behold the thing that is just.

Psalm 12. *Salvum me fac.*

For the end. A psalm of David, upon the eighth.

HELP me, Lord, for there is not one godly man
left; * for the faithful are minished from among
the children of men,

They talk of vanity every one with his
neighbour; * they do but flatter with their lips,
and dissemble in their double heart.

The Lord shall root out all deceitful lips, * and the
tongue that speaketh proud things;

Which have said, With our tongue will we
prevail; * we are they that ought to speak, who
is lord over us?

Now for the comfortless trouble's sake of the
needy, * and because of the deep sighing of the
poor,

I will up, saith the Lord; * and will help every one
from him that swelleth against him, and will set
him at rest.

The words of the Lord are pure words; * even as
the silver, which from the earth is tried, and
purified seven times in the fire.

Thou shalt keep them, O Lord; * thou shalt
 preserve him from this generation for ever.
The ungodly walk on every side: * when they are
 exalted, the children of men are put to rebuke.

Psalm 13. *Usquequo, Domine?*
For the end. A psalm of David.

How long wilt thou forget me, O Lord,
 for ever? * how long wilt thou hide thy face
 from me?
How long shall I seek counsel in my soul, and be
 so vexed in my heart? * how long shall mine
 enemies triumph over me?
Consider, and hear me, O Lord my God; * lighten
 mine eyes, that I sleep not in death.
Lest mine enemy say, I have prevailed against
 him: * for if I be cast down, they that trouble
 me will rejoice at it.
But my trust is in thy mercy, * and my heart is
 joyful in thy salvation.
I will sing of the Lord, because he hath dealt so
 lovingly with me; * yea, I will praise the Name
 of the Lord most Highest.

Psalm 14. *Dixit insipiens.*
For the end. A psalm of David.

THE fool hath said in his heart, * There is no God.

They are corrupt, and become abominable in their doings; * there is none that doeth good, no not one.

The Lord looked down from heaven upon the children of men; * to see if there were any that would understand, and seek after God.

But they are all gone out of the way, they are altogether become abominable; * there is none that doeth good, no not one.

Their throat is an open sepulchre; with their tongues have they deceived: * the poison of asps is under their lips.

Their mouth is full of cursing and bitterness; * their feet are swift to shed blood.

Destruction and unhappiness is in their ways, and the way of peace have they not known: * there is no fear of God before their eyes.

Have they no knowledge, that they are all such workers of mischief, * eating up my people as it were bread, and call not upon the Lord?

There were they brought in great fear, even where no fear was; * for God is in the generation of the righteous.

As for you, ye have made a mock at the counsel of the poor; * because he putteth his trust in the Lord.

Who shall give salvation unto Israel out of Sion? When the Lord turneth the captivity of his people, * then shall Jacob rejoice, and Israel shall be glad.

✠ THIRD STASIS ✠

Psalm 15. *Domine, quis habitabit?*
A psalm of David.

LORD, who shall dwell in thy tabernacle? * or who shall rest upon thy holy hill?

Even he that leadeth an uncorrupt life, * and doeth the thing which is right, and speaketh the truth from his heart.

He that hath used no deceit in his tongue, nor done evil to his neighbour, * and hath not slandered his neighbour.

He that setteth not by himself, but is lowly in his own eyes, * and maketh much of them that fear the Lord.

He that sweareth unto his neighbour, and disappointeth him not, * though it were to his own hindrance.

He that hath not given his money upon usury, * nor taken reward against the innocent.

Whoso doeth these things * shall never fall.

Psalm 16. *Conserva me, Domine.*
A writing of David.

PRESERVE me, O God; * for in thee have I put my trust.

O my soul, thou hast said unto the Lord, * Thou art my God, my goods are nothing unto thee.

All my delight is upon the saints, that are in the earth, * and upon such as excel in virtue.

But they that run after another god * shall have great trouble.

Their drink-offerings of blood will I not offer, * neither make mention of their names within my lips.

The Lord himself is the portion of mine
inheritance, and of my cup; * thou shalt
maintain my lot.
The lot is fallen unto me in a fair ground; * yea, I
have a goodly heritage.
I will thank the Lord for giving me warning; * my
reins also chasten me in the night-season.
I have set God always before me; * for he is on
my right hand, therefore I shall not fall.
Wherefore my heart was glad, and my glory
rejoiced: * my flesh also shall rest in hope.
For why? thou shalt not leave my soul in hell; *
neither shalt thou suffer thy Holy One to see
corruption.
Thou shalt shew me the path of life; in thy
presence is the fulness of joy, * and at thy right
hand there is pleasure for evermore.

Psalm 17. *Exaudi, Domine.*
A prayer of David.

HEAR the right, O Lord, consider my complaint, *
and hearken unto my prayer, that goeth not out
of feigned lips.

Let my sentence come forth from thy presence; *
and let thine eyes look upon the thing that is
equal.

Thou hast proved and visited mine heart in the
night-season; thou hast tried me, and shalt find
no wickedness in me; * for I am utterly
purposed that my mouth shall not offend.

Because of men's works, that are done against the
words of thy lips, * I have kept me from the
ways of the destroyer.

O hold thou up my goings in thy paths, * that my
footsteps slip not.

I have called upon thee, O God, for thou shalt hear
me: * incline thine ear to me, and hearken unto
my words.

Shew thy marvellous loving-kindness, thou that
art the Saviour of them which put their trust in
thee, * from such as resist thy right hand.

Keep me as the apple of an eye; * hide me under
the shadow of thy wings.

From the ungodly that trouble me; * mine enemies
compass me round about to take away my soul.

They are inclosed in their own fat, * and their
mouth speaketh proud things.

They lie waiting in our way on every side, *
turning their eyes down to the ground.

Like as a lion that is greedy of his prey, * and as it
were a lion's whelp, lurking in secret places.

Up, Lord, disappoint him, and cast him down; *
deliver my soul from the ungodly, which is a
sword of thine;

From the men of thy hand, O Lord, from the men,
I say, and from the evil world; * which have
their portion in this life, whose bellies thou
fillest with thy hid treasure.

They have children at their desire, * and leave the
rest of their substance for their babes.

But as for me, I will behold thy presence in
righteousness; * and when I awake up after thy
likeness, I shall be satisfied with it.

THE THIRD KATHISMA

✠ FIRST STASIS ✠

Psalm 18. *Diligam te, Domine.*

*For the end. A psalm of David, the servant of the
Lord. The words which he spake to the Lord, even
the words of this song, in the day in which the
Lord delivered him out of the hand of all his
enemies, and out of the hand of Saul. And he said:*

I WILL love thee, O Lord, my strength; the Lord is
my stony rock, and my defence; * my saviour,
my God, and my might, in whom I will trust,
my buckler, the horn also of my salvation, and
my refuge.

I will call upon the Lord, which is worthy to be
praised; * so shall I be safe from mine enemies.

The sorrows of death compassed me, * and the
overflowings of ungodliness made me afraid.

The pains of hell came about me; * the snares of
death overtook me.

In my trouble I will call upon the Lord, * and
complain unto my God.

So shall he hear my voice out of his holy temple, * and my complaint shall come before him, it shall enter even into his ears.

The earth trembled and quaked, * the very foundations also of the hills shook, and were removed, because he was wroth.

There went a smoke out in his presence, * and a consuming fire out of his mouth, so that coals were kindled at it.

He bowed the heavens also, and came down, * and it was dark under his feet.

He rode upon the cherubins, and did fly; * he came flying upon the wings of the wind.

He made darkness his secret place, * his pavilion round about him, with dark water and thick clouds to cover him.

At the brightness of his presence his clouds removed; * hail-stones, and coals of fire.

The Lord also thundered out of heaven, and the Highest gave his thunder; * hail-stones, and coals of fire.

He sent out his arrows, and scattered them; * he cast forth lightnings, and destroyed them.

The springs of water were seen, and the
foundations of the round world were
discovered, at thy chiding, O Lord, * at the
blasting of the breath of thy displeasure.
He shall send down from on high to fetch me, *
and shall take me out of many waters.
He shall deliver me from my strongest enemy, and
from them which hate me; * for they are too
mighty for me.
They prevented me in the day of my trouble; * but
the Lord was my upholder.
He brought me forth also into a place of liberty; *
he brought me forth, even because he had a
favour unto me.
The Lord shall reward me after my righteous
dealing: * according to the cleanness of my
hands shall he recompense me.
Because I have kept the ways of the Lord, * and
have not forsaken my God, as the wicked doth.
For I have an eye unto all his laws, * and will not
cast out his commandments from me.
I was also uncorrupt before him, * and eschewed
mine own wickedness.

Therefore shall the Lord reward me after my righteous dealing, * and according unto the cleanness of my hands in his eye-sight.

With the holy thou shalt be holy, * and with a perfect man thou shalt be perfect.

With the clean thou shalt be clean, * and with the froward thou shalt learn frowardness.

For thou shalt save the people that are in adversity, * and shalt bring down the high looks of the proud.

Thou also shalt light my candle; * the Lord my God shall make my darkness to be light.

For in thee I shall discomfit an host of men, * and with the help of my God I shall leap over the wall.

The way of God is an undefiled way; * the word of the Lord also is tried in the fire; he is the defender of all them that put their trust in him.

For who is God, but the Lord? * or who hath any strength, except our God?

It is God, that girdeth me with strength of war, * and maketh my way perfect.

He maketh my feet like harts' feet, * and setteth me up on high.

He teacheth mine hands to fight, * and mine arms
shall break even a bow of steel.
Thou hast given me the defence of thy salvation; *
thy right hand also shall hold me up, and thy
loving correction shall make me great.
Thou shalt make room enough under me for to
go, * that my footsteps shall not slide.
I will follow upon mine enemies, and overtake
them; * neither will I turn again till I have
destroyed them.
I will smite them, that they shall not be able to
stand, * but fall under my feet.
Thou hast girded me with strength unto the
battle; * thou shalt throw down mine enemies
under me.
Thou hast made mine enemies also to turn their
backs upon me, * and I shall destroy them that
hate me.
They shall cry, but there shall be none to help
them; * yea, even unto the Lord shall they cry,
but he shall not hear them.
I will beat them as small as the dust before the
wind: * I will cast them out as the clay in the
streets.

Thou shalt deliver me from the strivings of the
people, * and thou shalt make me the head of
the heathen.
A people whom I have not known * shall serve
me.
As soon as they hear of me, they shall obey me; *
but the strange children shall dissemble with
me.
The strange children shall fail, * and be afraid out
of their prisons.
The Lord liveth, and blessed be my strong
helper, * and praised be the Lord of my
salvation;
Even the God that seeth that I be avenged, * and
subdueth the people unto me.
It is he that delivereth me from my cruel enemies,
and setteth me up above mine adversaries: *
thou shalt rid me from the wicked man.
For this cause will I give thanks unto thee, O
Lord, among the Gentiles, * and sing praises
unto thy Name.
Great prosperity giveth he unto his King, * and
sheweth loving-kindness unto David his
Anointed, and unto his seed for evermore.

Psalm 19. *Cœli enarrant.*

For the end. A psalm of David.

THE heavens declare the glory of God; * and the firmament sheweth his handywork.

One day telleth another; * and one night certifieth another.

There is neither speech nor language; * but their voices are heard among them.

Their sound is gone out into all lands; * and their words into the ends of the world.

In them hath he set a tabernacle for the sun; * which cometh forth as a bridegroom out of his chamber, and rejoiceth as a giant to run his course.

It goeth forth from the uttermost part of the heaven, and runneth about unto the end of it again; * and there is nothing hid from the heat thereof.

The law of the Lord is an undefiled law, converting the soul; * the testimony of the Lord is sure, and giveth wisdom unto the simple.

The statutes of the Lord are right, and rejoice the
    heart; * the commandment of the Lord is pure,
    and giveth light unto the eyes.
The fear of the Lord is clean, and endureth for
    ever; * the judgements of the Lord are true, and
    righteous altogether.
More to be desired are they than gold, yea, than
    much fine gold; * sweeter also than honey, and
    the honey-comb.
Moreover, by them is thy servant taught; * and in
    keeping of them there is great reward.
Who can tell how oft he offendeth? * O cleanse
    thou me from my secret faults.
Keep thy servant also from presumptuous sins,
    lest they get the dominion over me; * so shall I
    be undefiled, and innocent from the great
    offence.
Let the words of my mouth, and the meditation of
    my heart, * be alway acceptable in thy sight,
O Lord, * my strength, and my redeemer.

Psalm 20. *Exaudiat te Dominus.*
For the end. A psalm of David.

THE Lord hear thee in the day of trouble; * the Name of the God of Jacob defend thee;

Send thee help from the sanctuary, * and strengthen thee out of Sion;

Remember all thy offerings, * and accept thy burnt-sacrifice;

Grant thee thy heart's desire, * and fulfil all thy mind.

We will rejoice in thy salvation, and triumph in the Name of the Lord our God: * the Lord perform all thy petitions.

Now know I that the Lord helpeth his Anointed, and will hear him from his holy heaven, * even with the wholesome strength of his right hand.

Some put their trust in chariots, and some in horses; * but we will remember the Name of the Lord our God.

They are brought down, and fallen; * but we are risen, and stand upright.

Save, Lord, and hear us, O King of heaven, * when we call upon thee.

Psalm 21. *Domine, in virtute tua.*
For the end. A psalm of David.

THE King shall rejoice in thy strength, O Lord; *
exceeding glad shall he be of thy salvation.

Thou hast given him his heart's desire, * and hast
not denied him the request of his lips.

For thou shalt prevent him with the blessings of
goodness, * and shalt set a crown of pure gold
upon his head.

He asked life of thee, and thou gavest him a long
life, * even for ever and ever.

His honour is great in thy salvation; * glory and
great worship shalt thou lay upon him.

For thou shalt give him everlasting felicity, * and
make him glad with the joy of thy countenance.

And why? because the King putteth his trust in the
Lord; * and in the mercy of the most Highest he
shall not miscarry.

All thine enemies shall feel thine hand; * thy right
hand shall find out them that hate thee.

Thou shalt make them like a fiery oven in time of
thy wrath: * the Lord shall destroy them in his
displeasure, and the fire shall consume them.

Their fruit shalt thou root out of the earth, * and
their seed from among the children of men.

For they intended mischief against thee, * and
imagined such a device as they are not able to
perform.

Therefore shalt thou put them to flight, * and the
strings of thy bow shalt thou make ready
against the face of them.

Be thou exalted, Lord, in thine own strength; * so
we will sing, and praise thy power.

✠ THIRD STASIS ✠

Psalm 22. *Deus, Deus meus.*

*For the end. A psalm of David concerning the
morning aid.*

MY GOD, my God, look upon me; why hast thou
forsaken me? * and art so far from my health,
and from the words of my complaint?

O my God, I cry in the day-time, but thou hearest
not; * and in the night-season also I take no
rest.

And thou continuest holy, * O thou worship of
Israel.

Our fathers hoped in thee; * they trusted in thee,
and thou didst deliver them.

They called upon thee, and were holpen; * they
put their trust in thee, and were not confounded.

But as for me, I am a worm, and no man; * a very
scorn of men, and the outcast of the people.

All they that see me laugh me to scorn; * they
shoot out their lips, and shake their heads,
saying,

He trusted in God, that he would deliver him; * let
him deliver him, if he will have him.

But thou art he that took me out of my mother's
womb; * thou wast my hope, when I hanged yet
upon my mother's breasts.

I have been left unto thee ever since I was born; *
thou art my God, even from my mother's
womb.

O go not from me, for trouble is hard at hand, *
and there is none to help me.

Many oxen are come about me; * fat bulls of
Basan close me in on every side.

They gape upon me with their mouths, * as it were
a ramping and a roaring lion.

I am poured out like water, and all my bones are
out of joint; * my heart also in the midst of my
body is even like melting wax.

My strength is dried up like a potsherd, and my
tongue cleaveth to my gums, * and thou shalt
bring me into the dust of death.

For many dogs are come about me, * and the
council of the wicked layeth siege against me.

They pierced my hands and my feet; I may tell all
my bones: * they stand staring and looking
upon me.

They part my garments among them, * and casts
lots upon my vesture.

But be not thou far from me, O Lord; * thou art
my succour, haste thee to help me.

Deliver my soul from the sword, * my darling
from the power of the dog.

Save me from the lion's mouth; * thou hast heard
me also from among the horns of the unicorns.

I will declare thy Name unto my brethren; * in the
midst of the congregation will I praise thee.

O praise the Lord, ye that fear him: * magnify
him, all ye of the seed of Jacob, and fear him,
all ye seed of Israel.

For he hath not despised, nor abhorred, the low
  estate of the poor; * he hath not hid his face
  from him, but when he called unto him he heard
  him.
My praise is of thee in the great congregation; *
  my vows will I perform in the sight of them that
  fear him.
The poor shall eat and be satisfied; * they that
  seek after the Lord shall praise him; your heart
  shall live for ever.
All the ends of the world shall remember
  themselves, and be turned unto the Lord; * and
  all the kindreds of the nations shall worship
  before him.
For the kingdom is the Lord's, * and he is the
  Governor among the people.
All such as be fat upon earth * have eaten, and
  worshipped.
All they that go down into the dust shall kneel
  before him; * and no man hath quickened his
  own soul.
My seed shall serve him: * they shall be counted
  unto the Lord for a generation.

They shall come, and the heavens shall declare his
  righteousness * unto a people that shall be born,
  whom the Lord hath made.

Psalm 23. *Dominus regit me.*
A psalm of David.

THE Lord is my shepherd; * therefore can I lack
  nothing.

He shall feed me in a green pasture, * and lead me
  forth beside the waters of comfort.

He shall convert my soul, * and bring me forth in
  the paths of righteousness, for his Name's sake.

Yea, though I walk through the valley of the
  shadow of death, I will fear no evil; * for thou
  art with me; thy rod and thy staff comfort me.

Thou shalt prepare a table before me against them
  that trouble me; * thou hast anointed my head
  with oil, and my cup shall be full.

But thy loving-kindness and mercy shall follow
  me all the days of my life; * and I will dwell in
  the house of the Lord for ever.

Psalm 24. *Domini est terra.*

A psalm of David on the first day of the week.

THE earth is the Lord's, and all that therein is; *
the compass of the world, and they that dwell
therein.

For he hath founded it upon the seas, * and
prepared it upon the floods.

Who shall ascend into the hill of the Lord? * or
who shall rise up in his holy place?

Even he that hath clean hands, and a pure heart; *
and that hath not lift up his mind unto vanity,
nor sworn to deceive his neighbour.

He shall receive the blessing from the Lord, * and
righteousness from the God of his salvation.

This is the generation of them that seek him; *
even of them that seek thy face, O Jacob.

Lift up your heads, O ye gates, and be ye lift up,
ye everlasting doors; * and the King of glory
shall come in.

Who is the King of glory? * it is the Lord strong
and mighty, even the Lord mighty in battle.

Lift up your heads, O ye gates, and be ye lift up,
  ye everlasting doors; * and the King of glory
  shall come in.
Who is the King of glory? * even the Lord of
  hosts, he is the King of glory.

THE FOURTH KATHISMA

✠ FIRST STASIS ✠

Psalm 25. *Ad te, Domine, levavi.*
A psalm of David.

UNTO thee, O Lord, will I lift up my soul; my
God, I have put my trust in thee: * O let me not
be confounded, neither let mine enemies
triumph over me.

For all they that hope in thee shall not be
ashamed; * but such as transgress without a
cause shall be put to confusion.

Shew me thy ways, O Lord, * and teach me thy
paths.

Lead me forth in thy truth, and learn me: * for
thou art the God of my salvation; in thee hath
been my hope all the day long.

Call to remembrance, O Lord, thy tender
mercies, * and thy loving-kindnesses, which
have been ever of old.

O remember not the sins and offences of my
youth; * but according to thy mercy think thou
upon me, O Lord, for thy goodness.

Gracious and righteous is the Lord; * therefore
will he teach sinners in the way.

Them that are meek shall he guide in judgement; *
and such as are gentle, them shall he learn his
way.

All the paths of the Lord are mercy and truth, *
unto such as keep his covenant and his
testimonies.

For thy Name's sake, O Lord, * be merciful unto
my sin, for it is great.

What man is he that feareth the Lord? * him shall
he teach in the way that he shall choose.

His soul shall dwell at ease, * and his seed shall
inherit the land.

The secret of the Lord is among them that fear
him; * and he will shew them his covenant.

Mine eyes are ever looking unto the Lord; * for he
shall pluck my feet out of the net.

Turn thee unto me, and have mercy upon me; *
for I am desolate and in misery.

The sorrows of my heart are enlarged: * O bring thou me out of my troubles.

Look upon my adversity and misery, * and forgive me all my sin.

Consider mine enemies, how many they are; * and they bear a tyrannous hate against me.

O keep my soul, and deliver me: * let me not be confounded, for I have put my trust in thee.

Let perfectness and righteous dealing wait upon me; * for my hope hath been in thee.

Deliver Israel, O God, * out of all his troubles.

Psalm 26. *Judica me, Domine.*
A psalm of David.

BE THOU my judge, O Lord, for I have walked innocently: * my trust hath been also in the Lord, therefore shall I not fall.

Examine me, O Lord, and prove me; * try out my reins and my heart.

For thy loving-kindness is ever before mine eyes; * and I will walk in thy truth.

I have not dwelt with vain persons; * neither will I have fellowship with the deceitful.

I have hated the congregation of the wicked; * and
will not sit among the ungodly.

I will wash my hands in innocency, O Lord; * and
so will I go to thine altar.

That I may shew the voice of thanksgiving, * and
tell of all thy wondrous works.

Lord, I have loved the habitation of thy house, *
and the place where thine honour dwelleth.

O shut not up my soul with the sinners, * nor my
life with the blood-thirsty.

In whose hands is wickedness, * and their right
hand is full of gifts.

But as for me, I will walk innocently: * O deliver
me, and be merciful unto me.

My foot standeth right: * I will praise the Lord in
the congregations.

Psalm 27. *Dominus illuminatio.*

A psalm of David before he was anointed.

THE Lord is my light and my salvation; whom
then shall I fear? * the Lord is the strength of
my life; of whom then shall I be afraid?

When the wicked, even mine enemies and my
    foes, came upon me to eat up my flesh, * they
    stumbled and fell.
Though an host of men were laid against me, yet
    shall not my heart be afraid; * and though there
    rose up war against me, yet will I put my trust
    in him.
One thing have I desired of the Lord, which I will
    require; * even that I may dwell in the house of
    the Lord all the days of my life, to behold the
    fair beauty of the Lord, and to visit his temple.
For in the time of trouble he shall hide me in his
    tabernacle; * yea, in the secret place of his
    dwelling shall he hide me, and set me up upon a
    rock of stone.
And now shall he lift up mine head * above mine
    enemies round about me.
Therefore will I offer in his dwelling an oblation
    with great gladness: * I will sing, and speak
    praises unto the Lord.
Hearken unto my voice, O Lord, when I cry unto
    thee; * have mercy upon me, and hear me.
My heart hath talked of thee, Seek ye my face: *
    Thy face, Lord, will I seek.

O hide not thou thy face from me, * nor cast thy
   servant away in displeasure.
Thou hast been my succour; * leave me not,
   neither forsake me, O God of my salvation.
When my father and my mother forsake me, * the
   Lord taketh me up.
Teach me thy way, O Lord, * and lead me in the
   right way, because of mine enemies.
Deliver me not over into the will of mine
   adversaries: * for there are false witnesses risen
   up against me, and such as speak wrong.
I should utterly have fainted, * but that I believe
   verily to see the goodness of the Lord in the
   land of the living.
O tarry thou the Lord's leisure; * be strong, and he
   shall comfort thine heart; and put thou thy trust
   in the Lord.

Psalm 28. *Ad te, Domine.*
A psalm of David.

UNTO thee will I cry, O Lord my strength: * think no scorn of me; lest, if thou make as though thou hearest not, I become like them that go down into the pit.

Hear the voice of my humble petitions, when I cry unto thee; * when I hold up my hands towards the mercy-seat of thy holy temple.

O pluck me not away, neither destroy me, with the ungodly and wicked doers, * which speak friendly to their neighbours, but imagine mischief in their hearts.

Reward them according to their deeds, * and according to the wickedness of their own inventions.

Recompense them after the work of their hands; * pay them that they have deserved.

For they regard not in their mind the works of the Lord, nor the operation of his hands; * therefore shall he break them down, and not build them up.

Praised be the Lord; * for he hath heard the voice of my humble petitions.

The Lord is my strength and my shield; my heart hath trusted in him, and I am helped; * therefore my heart danceth for joy, and in my song will I praise him.

The Lord is my strength, * and he is the wholesome defence of his Anointed.

O save thy people, and give thy blessing unto thine inheritance: * feed them, and set them up for ever.

Psalm 29. *Afferte Domino.*

A psalm of David on the occasion of the solemn assembly of the Tabernacle.

BRING unto the Lord, O ye mighty, bring young rams unto the Lord, * ascribe unto the Lord worship and strength.

Give the Lord the honour due unto his Name; * worship the Lord with holy worship.

It is the Lord that commandeth the waters; * it is the glorious God that maketh the thunder.

It is the Lord that ruleth the sea; the voice of the
Lord is mighty in operation; * the voice of the
Lord is a glorious voice.

The voice of the Lord breaketh the cedar-trees; *
yea, the Lord breaketh the cedars of Libanus.

He maketh them also to skip like a calf; * Libanus
also, and Sirion, like a young unicorn.

The voice of the Lord divideth the flames of fire;
the voice of the Lord shaketh the wilderness; *
yea, the Lord shaketh the wilderness of Cades.

The voice of the Lord maketh the hinds to bring
forth young, and discovereth the thick bushes: *
in his temple doth every man speak of his
honour.

The Lord sitteth above the water-flood, * and the
Lord remaineth a King for ever.

The Lord shall give strength unto his people; * the
Lord shall give his people the blessing of peace.

Psalm 30. *Exaltabo te, Domine.*

*For the end. A psalm of a song at the dedication
of the house of David.*

I WILL magnify thee, O Lord, for thou hast set me
up, * and not made my foes to triumph over me.

O Lord my God, I cried unto thee; * and thou hast
   healed me.
Thou, Lord, hast brought my soul out of hell: *
   thou hast kept my life from them that go down
   to the pit.
Sing praises unto the Lord, O ye saints of his; *
   and give thanks unto him for a remembrance of
   his holiness.
For his wrath endureth but the twinkling of an
   eye, and in his pleasure is life; * heaviness may
   endure for a night, but joy cometh in the
   morning.
And in my prosperity I said, I shall never be
   removed: * thou, Lord, of thy goodness hast
   made my hill so strong.
Thou didst turn thy face from me, * and I was
   troubled.
Then cried I unto thee, O Lord; * and gat me to
   my Lord right humbly.
What profit is there in my blood, * when I go
   down to the pit?
Shall the dust give thanks unto thee? * or shall it
   declare thy truth?

Hear, O Lord, and have mercy upon me; * Lord,
be thou my helper.

Thou hast turned my heaviness into joy; * thou
hast put off my sackcloth, and girded me with
gladness.

Therefore shall every good man sing of thy praise
without ceasing. * O my God, I will give thanks
unto thee for ever.

✠ THIRD STASIS ✠

Psalm 31. *In te, Domine, speravi.*
*For the end. A psalm of David; an utterance of
extreme fear.*

IN THEE, O Lord, have I put my trust, let me never
be put to confusion; * deliver me in thy
righteousness.

Bow down thine ear to me; * make haste to
deliver me.

And be thou my strong rock, and house of
defence, * that thou mayest save me.

For thou art my strong rock, and my castle: * be
thou also my guide, and lead me for thy Name's
sake.

Draw me out of the net that they have laid privily
for me; * for thou art my strength.

Into thy hands I commend my spirit; * for thou
hast redeemed me, O Lord, thou God of truth.

I have hated them that hold of superstitious
vanities, * and my trust hath been in the Lord.

I will be glad and rejoice in thy mercy; * for thou
hast considered my trouble, and hast known my
soul in adversities.

Thou hast not shut me up into the hand of the
enemy; * but hast set my feet in a large room.

Have mercy upon me, O Lord, for I am in
trouble, * and mine eye is consumed for very
heaviness; yea, my soul and my body.

For my life is waxen old with heaviness, * and my
years with mourning.

My strength faileth me, because of mine
iniquity, * and my bones are consumed.

I became a reproof among all mine enemies, but
especially among my neighbours; * and they of
mine acquaintance were afraid of me; and they

that did see me without conveyed themselves from me.

I am clean forgotten, as a dead man out of mind; * I am become like a broken vessel.

For I have heard the blasphemy of the multitude, and fear is on every side; * while they conspire together against me, and take their counsel to take away my life.

But my hope hath been in thee, O Lord; * I have said, Thou art my God.

My time is in thy hand; deliver me from the hand of mine enemies, * and from them that persecute me.

Shew thy servant the light of thy countenance, * and save me for thy mercy's sake.

Let me not be confounded, O Lord, for I have called upon thee; * let the ungodly be put to confusion, and be put to silence in the grave.

Let the lying lips be put to silence, * which cruelly, disdainfully, and despitefully, speak against the righteous.

O how plentiful is thy goodness, which thou hast
    laid up for them that fear thee, * and that thou
    hast prepared for them that put their trust in
    thee, even before the sons of men!

Thou shalt hide them privily by thine own
    presence from the provoking of all men: * thou
    shalt keep them secretly in thy tabernacle from
    the strife of tongues.

Thanks be to the Lord; * for he hath shewed me
    marvellous great kindness in a strong city.

And when I made haste, I said, * I am cast out of
    the sight of thine eyes.

Nevertheless, thou heardest the voice of my
    prayer, * when I cried unto thee.

O love the Lord, all ye his saints; * for the Lord
    preserveth them that are faithful, and
    plenteously rewardeth the proud doer.

Be strong, and he shall establish your heart, * all
    ye that put your trust in the Lord.

Psalm 32. *Beati, quorum.*
A psalm of instruction by David.

BLESSED is he whose unrighteousness is
    forgiven, * and whose sin is covered.

Blessed is the man unto whom the Lord imputeth
    no sin, * and in whose spirit there is no guile.

For while I held my tongue, * my bones
    consumed away through my daily complaining.

For thy hand is heavy upon me day and night, *
    and my moisture is like the drought in summer.

I will acknowledge my sin unto thee; * and mine
    unrighteousness have I not hid.

I said, I will confess my sins unto the Lord; * and
    so thou forgavest the wickedness of my sin.

For this shall every one that is godly make his
    prayer unto thee, in a time when thou mayest be
    found; * but in the great water-floods they shall
    not come nigh him.

Thou art a place to hide me in, thou shalt preserve
    me from trouble; * thou shalt compass me
    about with songs of deliverance.

I will inform thee, and teach thee in the way
    wherein thou shalt go; * and I will guide thee
    with mine eye.

Be ye not like to horse and mule, which have no
  understanding; * whose mouths must be held
  with bit and bridle, lest they fall upon thee.
Great plagues remain for the ungodly; * but
  whoso putteth his trust in the Lord, mercy
  embraceth him on every side.
Be glad, O ye righteous, and rejoice in the Lord; *
  and be joyful, all ye that are true of heart.

THE FIFTH KATHISMA

✠ FIRST STASIS ✠

Psalm 33. *Exultate, justi.*
A psalm of David.

REJOICE in the Lord, O ye righteous; * for it
  becometh well the just to be thankful.

Praise the Lord with harp; * sing praises unto him
  with the lute, and instrument of ten strings.

Sing unto the Lord a new song; * sing praises
  lustily unto him with a good courage.

For the word of the Lord is true; * and all his
  works are faithful.

He loveth righteousness and judgement; * the
  earth is full of the goodness of the Lord.

By the word of the Lord were the heavens made; *
  and all the hosts of them by the breath of his
  mouth.

He gathereth the waters of the sea together, as it
  were upon an heap; * and layeth up the deep, as
  in a treasure-house.

Let all the earth fear the Lord: * stand in awe of
him, all ye that dwell in the world.

For he spake, and it was done; * he commanded,
and it stood fast.

The Lord bringeth the counsel of the heathen to
nought, * and maketh the devices of the people
to be of none effect, and casteth out the
counsels of princes.

The counsel of the Lord shall endure for ever, *
and the thoughts of his heart from generation to
generation.

Blessed are the people, whose God is the Lord
Jehovah; * and blessed are the folk, that he hath
chosen to him to be his inheritance.

The Lord looked down from heaven, and beheld
all the children of men; * from the habitation of
his dwelling he considereth all them that dwell
on the earth.

He fashioneth all the hearts of them, * and
understandeth all their works.

There is no king that can be saved by the
multitude of an host; * neither is any mighty
man delivered by much strength.

A horse is counted but a vain thing to save a man; * neither shall he deliver any man by his great strength.

Behold, the eye of the Lord is upon them that fear him; * and upon them that put their trust in his mercy;

To deliver their soul from death, * and to feed them in the time of dearth.

Our soul hath patiently tarried for the Lord; * for he is our help and our shield.

For our heart shall rejoice in him; * because we have hoped in his holy Name.

Let thy merciful kindness, O Lord, be upon us, * like as we do put our trust in thee.

Psalm 34. *Benedicam Domino.*
A psalm of David, when he changed his countenance before Abimelech, and he was dismissed and departed.

I WILL alway give thanks unto the Lord; * his praise shall ever be in my mouth.

My soul shall make her boast in the Lord; * the humble shall hear thereof, and be glad.

O praise the Lord with me, * and let us magnify
his Name together.

I sought the Lord, and he heard me; * yea, he
delivered me out of all my fear.

They had an eye unto him, and were lightened; *
and their faces were not ashamed.

Lo, the poor crieth, and the Lord heareth him; *
yea, and saveth him out of all his troubles.

The angel of the Lord tarrieth round about them
that fear him, * and delivereth them.

O taste, and see, how gracious the Lord is: *
blessed is the man that trusteth in him.

O fear the Lord, ye that are his saints; * for they
that fear him lack nothing.

The lions do lack, and suffer hunger; * but they
who seek the Lord shall want no manner of
thing that is good.

Come, ye children, and hearken unto me; * I will
teach you the fear of the Lord.

What man is he that lusteth to live, * and would
fain see good days?

Keep thy tongue from evil, * and thy lips, that
they speak no guile.

Eschew evil, and do good; * seek peace, and
ensue it.

The eyes of the Lord are over the righteous, * and
his ears are open unto their prayers.

The countenance of the Lord is against them that
do evil, * to root out the remembrance of them
from the earth.

The righteous cry, and the Lord heareth them, *
and delivereth them out of all their troubles.

The Lord is nigh unto them that are of a contrite
heart, * and will save such as be of an humble
spirit.

Great are the troubles of the righteous; * but the
Lord delivereth him out of all.

He keepeth all his bones, * so that not one of them
is broken.

But misfortune shall slay the ungodly; * and they
that hate the righteous shall be desolate.

The Lord delivereth the souls of his servants; *
and all they that put their trust in him shall not
be destitute.

Psalm 35. *Judica, Domine.*
A psalm of David.

PLEAD thou my cause, O Lord, with them that
strive with me, * and fight thou against them
that fight against me.

Lay hand upon the shield and buckler, * and stand
up to help me.

Bring forth the spear, and stop the way against
them that persecute me: * say unto my soul, I
am thy salvation.

Let them be confounded and put to shame, that
seek after my soul; * let them be turned back
and brought to confusion, that imagine mischief
for me.

Let them be as the dust before the wind, * and the
angel of the Lord scattering them.

Let their way be dark and slippery, * and let the
angel of the Lord persecute them.

For they have privily laid their net to destroy me
without a cause; * yea, even without a cause
have they made a pit for my soul.

Let a sudden destruction come upon him unawares, and his net, that he hath laid privily, catch himself; * that he may fall into his own mischief.

And, my soul, be joyful in the Lord; * it shall rejoice in his salvation.

All my bones shall say, Lord, who is like unto thee, who deliverest the poor from him that is too strong for him; * yea, the poor, and him that is in misery, from him that spoileth him?

False witnesses did rise up: * they laid to my charge things that I knew not.

They rewarded me evil for good, * to the great discomfort of my soul.

Nevertheless, when they were sick, I put on sackcloth, and humbled my soul with fasting; * and my prayer shall turn into mine own bosom.

I behaved myself as though it had been my friend or my brother; * I went heavily, as one that mourneth for his mother.

But in mine adversity they rejoiced, and gathered themselves together; * yea, the very abjects came together against me unawares, making mouths at me, and ceased not.

With the flatterers were busy mockers, * who gnashed upon me with their teeth.

Lord, how long wilt thou look upon this? * O deliver my soul from the calamities which they bring on me, and my darling from the lions.

So will I give thee thanks in the great congregation; * I will praise thee among much people.

O let not them that are mine enemies triumph over me ungodly; * neither let them wink with their eyes that hate me without a cause.

And why? their communing is not for peace; * but they imagine deceitful words against them that are quiet in the land.

They gaped upon me with their mouths, and said, * Fie on thee, fie on thee, we saw it with our eyes.

This thou hast seen, O Lord; * hold not thy tongue then, go not far from me, O Lord.

Awake, and stand up to judge my quarrel; * avenge thou my cause, my God, and my Lord.

Judge me, O Lord my God, according to thy righteousness; * and let them not triumph over me.

Let them not say in their hearts, There, there, so
would we have it; * neither let them say, We
have devoured him.
Let them be put to confusion and shame together,
that rejoice at my trouble; * let them be clothed
with rebuke and dishonour, that boast
themselves against me.
Let them be glad and rejoice, that favour my
righteous dealing; * yea, let them say alway,
Blessed be the Lord, who hath pleasure in the
prosperity of his servant.
And as for my tongue, it shall be talking of thy
righteousness, * and of thy praise all the day
long.

Psalm 36. *Dixit injustus.*
For the end. By David the servant of the Lord.
MY HEART sheweth me the wickedness of the
ungodly, * that there is no fear of God before
his eyes.
For he flattereth himself in his own sight, * until
his abominable sin be found out.

The words of his mouth are unrighteous, and full
of deceit: * he hath left off to behave himself
wisely, and to do good.

He imagineth mischief upon his bed, and hath set
himself in no good way; * neither doth he abhor
any thing that is evil.

Thy mercy, O Lord, reacheth unto the heavens, *
and thy faithfulness unto the clouds.

Thy righteousness standeth like the strong
mountains: * thy judgements are like the great
deep.

Thou, Lord, shalt save both man and beast; How
excellent is thy mercy, O God! * and the
children of men shall put their trust under the
shadow of thy wings.

They shall be satisfied with the plenteousness of
thy house; * and thou shalt give them drink of
thy pleasures, as out of the river.

For with thee is the well of life; * and in thy light
shall we see light.

O continue forth thy loving-kindness unto them
that know thee, * and thy righteousness unto
them that are true of heart.

O let not the foot of pride come against me; * and
    let not the hand of the ungodly cast me down.
There are they fallen, all that work wickedness: *
    they are cast down, and shall not be able to
    stand.

✠ THIRD STASIS ✠

Psalm 37. *Noli æmulari.*
A psalm of David.

FRET not thyself because of the ungodly; * neither
    be thou envious against the evil-doers.
For they shall soon be cut down like the grass, *
    and be withered even as the green herb.
Put thou thy trust in the Lord, and be doing
    good; * dwell in the land, and verily thou shalt
    be fed.
Delight thou in the Lord, * and he shall give thee
    thy heart's desire.
Commit thy way unto the Lord, and put thy trust
    in him, * and he shall bring it to pass.
He shall make thy righteousness as clear as the
    light, * and thy just dealing as the noon-day.

Hold thee still in the Lord, and abide patiently upon him: * but grieve not thyself at him whose way doth prosper, against the man that doeth after evil counsels.

Leave off from wrath, and let go displeasure: * fret not thyself, else shalt thou be moved to do evil.

Wicked doers shall be rooted out; * and they that patiently abide the Lord, those shall inherit the land.

Yet a little while, and the ungodly shall be clean gone: * thou shalt look after his place, and he shall be away.

But the meek-spirited shall possess the earth, * and shall be refreshed in the multitude of peace.

The ungodly seeketh counsel against the just, * and gnasheth upon him with his teeth.

The Lord shall laugh him to scorn; * for he hath seen that his day is coming.

The ungodly have drawn out the sword, and have bent their bow, * to cast down the poor and needy, and to slay such as are of a right conversation.

Their sword shall go through their own heart, *
and their bow shall be broken.

A small thing that the righteous hath, * is better
than great riches of the ungodly.

For the arms of the ungodly shall be broken, * and
the Lord upholdeth the righteous.

The Lord knoweth the days of the godly; * and
their inheritance shall endure for ever.

They shall not be confounded in the perilous
time; * and in the days of dearth they shall have
enough.

As for the ungodly, they shall perish; and the
enemies of the Lord shall consume as the fat of
lambs: * yea, even as the smoke shall they
consume away.

The ungodly borroweth, and payeth not again; *
but the righteous is merciful and liberal.

Such as are blessed of God shall possess the
land; * and they that are cursed of him shall be
rooted out.

The Lord ordereth a good man's going, * and
maketh his way acceptable to himself.

Though he fall, he shall not be cast away; * for the
Lord upholdeth him with his hand.

I have been young, and now am old; * and yet saw
  I never the righteous forsaken, nor his seed
  begging their bread.
The righteous is ever merciful, and lendeth; * and
  his seed is blessed.
Flee from evil, and do the thing that is good; * and
  dwell for evermore.
For the Lord loveth the thing that is right; * he
  forsaketh not his that be godly, but they are
  preserved for ever.
The unrighteous shall be punished; * as for the
  seed of the ungodly, it shall be rooted out.
The righteous shall inherit the land, * and dwell
  therein for ever.
The mouth of the righteous is exercised in
  wisdom, * and his tongue will be talking of
  judgement.
The law of his God is in his heart, * and his
  goings shall not slide.
The ungodly seeth the righteous, * and seeketh
  occasion to slay him.
The Lord will not leave him in his hand, * nor
  condemn him when he is judged.

Hope thou in the Lord, and keep his way, and he shall promote thee, that thou shalt possess the land: * when the ungodly shall perish, thou shalt see it.

I myself have seen the ungodly in great power, * and flourishing like a green bay-tree.

I went by, and lo, he was gone: * I sought him, but his place could no where be found.

Keep innocency, and take heed unto the thing that is right; * for that shall bring a man peace at the last.

As for the transgressors, they shall perish together; * and the end of the ungodly is, they shall be rooted out at the last.

But the salvation of the righteous cometh of the Lord; * who is also their strength in the time of trouble.

And the Lord shall stand by them, and save them; * he shall deliver them from the ungodly, and shall save them, because they put their trust in him.

THE SIXTH KATHISMA

✠ FIRST STASIS ✠

Psalm 38. *Domine, ne in furore.*

A psalm of David. For remembrance concerning the Sabbath-day.

PUT me not to rebuke, O Lord, in thine anger; *
neither chasten me in thy heavy displeasure.

For thine arrows stick fast in me, * and thy hand
presseth me sore.

There is no health in my flesh, because of thy
displeasure; * neither is there any rest in my
bones, by reason of my sin.

For my wickednesses are gone over my head, *
and are like a sore burden, too heavy for me to
bear.

My wounds stink, and are corrupt, * through my
foolishness.

I am brought into so great trouble and misery, *
that I go mourning all the day long.

For my loins are filled with a sore disease, * and
there is no whole part in my body.

I am feeble, and sore smitten; * I have roared for
the very disquietness of my heart.

Lord, thou knowest all my desire; * and my
groaning is not hid from thee.

My heart panteth, my strength hath failed me, *
and the sight of mine eyes is gone from me.

My lovers and my neighbours did stand looking
upon my trouble, * and my kinsmen stood afar
off.

They also that sought after my life laid snares for
me; * and they that went about to do me evil
talked of wickedness, and imagined deceit all
the day long.

As for me, I was like a deaf man, and heard not; *
and as one that is dumb, who doth not open his
mouth.

I became even as a man that heareth not, * and in
whose mouth are no reproofs.

For in thee, O Lord, have I put my trust; * thou
shalt answer for me, O Lord my God.

I have required that they, even mine enemies,
should not triumph over me; * for when my
foot slipped, they rejoiced greatly against me.

And I, truly, am set in the plague, * and my
heaviness is ever in my sight.
For I will confess my wickedness, * and be sorry
for my sin.
But mine enemies live, and are mighty; * and they
that hate me wrongfully are many in number.
They also that reward evil for good are against
me; * because I follow the thing that good is.
Forsake me not, O Lord my God; * be not thou far
from me.
Haste thee to help me, * O Lord God of my
salvation.

Psalm 39. *Dixi, Custodiam.*
For the end. A song of David, for Idithun.

I SAID, I will take heed to my ways, * that I offend
not in my tongue.
I will keep my mouth as it were with a bridle, *
while the ungodly is in my sight.
I held my tongue, and spake nothing: * I kept
silence, yea, even from good words; but it was
pain and grief to me.

My heart was hot within me, and while I was thus
musing the fire kindled, * and at the last I spake
with my tongue;

Lord, let me know mine end, and the number of
my days; * that I may be certified how long I
have to live.

Behold, thou hast made my days as it were a span
long, and mine age is even as nothing in respect
of thee; * and verily every man living is
altogether vanity.

For man walketh in a vain shadow, and
disquieteth himself in vain; * he heapeth up
riches, and cannot tell who shall gather them.

And now, Lord, what is my hope? * truly my hope
is even in thee.

Deliver me from all mine offences; * and make
me not a rebuke unto the foolish.

I became dumb, and opened not my mouth; * for
it was thy doing.

Take thy plague away from me: * I am even
consumed by the means of thy heavy hand.

When thou with rebukes dost chasten man for sin, thou makest his beauty to consume away, like as it were a moth fretting a garment: * every man therefore is but vanity.

Hear my prayer, O Lord, and with thine ears consider my calling; * hold not thy peace at my tears.

For I am a stranger with thee, and a sojourner, * as all my fathers were.

O spare me a little, that I may recover my strength, * before I go hence, and be no more seen.

Psalm 40. *Expectans expectavi.*
For the end. A psalm of David.

I WAITED patiently for the Lord, * and he inclined unto me, and heard my calling.

He brought me also out of the horrible pit, out of the mire and clay, * and set my feet upon the rock, and ordered my goings.

And he hath put a new song in my mouth, * even a thanksgiving unto our God.

Many shall see it, and fear, * and shall put their trust in the Lord.

Blessed is the man that hath set his hope in the
    Lord, * and turned not unto the proud, and to
    such as go about with lies.
O Lord my God, great are the wondrous works
    which thou hast done, like as be also thy
    thoughts which are to us-ward; * and yet there
    is no man that ordereth them unto thee:
If I should declare them, and speak of them, *
    they should be more than I am able to express.
Sacrifice and meat-offering thou wouldest not, *
    but mine ears hast thou opened.
Burnt-offerings, and sacrifice for sin, hast thou not
    required: * then said I, Lo, I come,
In the volume of the book it is written of me, that I
    should fulfil thy will, O my God: * I am content
    to do it; yea, thy law is within my heart.
I have declared thy righteousness in the great
    congregation: * lo, I will not refrain my lips, O
    Lord, and that thou knowest.
I have not hid thy righteousness within my
    heart; * my talk hath been of thy truth and of
    thy salvation.
I have not kept back thy loving mercy and truth *
    from the great congregation.

Withdraw not thou thy mercy from me, O Lord; *
let thy loving-kindness and thy truth alway
preserve me.

For innumerable troubles are come about me; my
sins have taken such hold upon me that I am not
able to look up; * yea, they are more in number
than the hairs of my head, and my heart hath
failed me.

O Lord, let it be thy pleasure to deliver me; *
make haste, O Lord, to help me.

Let them be ashamed and confounded together,
that seek after my soul to destroy it; * let them
be driven backward and put to rebuke, that wish
me evil.

Let them be desolate, and rewarded with shame, *
that say unto me, Fie upon thee, fie upon thee.

Let all those that seek thee be joyful and glad in
thee; * and let such as love thy salvation say
alway, The Lord be praised.

As for me, I am poor and needy; * but the Lord
careth for me.

Thou art my helper and redeemer; * make no long
tarrying, O my God.

Psalm 41. *Beatus qui intelligit.*
For the end. A psalm of David.

BLESSED is he that considereth the poor and
needy; * the Lord shall deliver him in the time
of trouble.

The Lord preserve him, and keep him alive, that
he may be blessed upon earth; * and deliver not
thou him into the will of his enemies.

The Lord comfort him, when he lieth sick upon
his bed; * make thou all his bed in his sickness.

I said, Lord, be merciful unto me; * heal my soul,
for I have sinned against thee.

Mine enemies speak evil of me, * When shall he
die, and his name perish?

And if he come to see me, he speaketh vanity, *
and his heart conceiveth falsehood within
himself, and when he cometh forth he telleth it.

All mine enemies whisper together against me; *
even against me do they imagine this evil.

Let the sentence of guiltiness proceed against
him; * and now that he lieth, let him rise up no
more.

Yea, even mine own familiar friend, whom I
trusted, * who did also eat of my bread, hath
laid great wait for me.
But be thou merciful unto me, O Lord; * raise
thou me up again, and I shall reward them.
By this I know thou favourest me, * that mine
enemy doth not triumph against me.
And when I am in my health, thou upholdest
me, * and shalt set me before thy face for ever.
Blessed be the Lord God of Israel, * world
without end. Amen.

Psalm 42. *Quemadmodum.*

*For the end. A psalm for instruction, for the sons
of Core.*

LIKE as the hart desireth the water-brooks, * so
longeth my soul after thee, O God.
My soul is athirst for God, yea, even for the living
God: * when shall I come to appear before the
presence of God?
My tears have been my meat day and night, *
while they daily say unto me, Where is now thy
God?

Now when I think thereupon, I pour out my heart by myself; * for I went with the multitude, and brought them forth into the house of God;

In the voice of praise and thanksgiving, * among such as keep holy-day.

Why art thou so full of heaviness, O my soul, * and why art thou so disquieted within me?

Put thy trust in God; * for I will yet give him thanks for the help of his countenance.

My God, my soul is vexed within me; * therefore will I remember thee concerning the land of Jordan, and the little hill of Hermon.

One deep calleth another, because of the noise of the water-pipes; * all thy waves and storms are gone over me.

The Lord hath granted his loving-kindness in the day-time; * and in the night-season did I sing of him, and made my prayer unto the God of my life.

I will say unto the God of my strength, Why hast thou forgotten me? * why go I thus heavily, while the enemy oppresseth me?

My bones are smitten asunder as with a sword, *
while mine enemies that trouble me cast me in
the teeth;

Namely, while they say daily unto me, * Where is
now thy God?

Why art thou so vexed, O my soul? * and why art
thou so disquieted within me?

O put thy trust in God; * for I will yet thank him,
which is the help of my countenance, and my
God.

Psalm 43. *Judica me, Deus.*
A psalm of David.

GIVE sentence with me, O God, and defend my
cause against the ungodly people; * O deliver
me from the deceitful and wicked man.

For thou art the God of my strength, why hast
thou put me from thee? * and why go I so
heavily, while the enemy oppresseth me?

O send out thy light and thy truth, that they may
lead me, * and bring me unto thy holy hill, and
to thy dwelling.

And that I may go unto the altar of God, even unto the God of my joy and gladness; * and upon the harp will I give thanks unto thee, O God, my God.

Why art thou so heavy, O my soul? * and why art thou so disquieted within me?

O put thy trust in God; * for I will yet give him thanks, which is the help of my countenance, and my God.

✠ THIRD STASIS ✠

Psalm 44. *Deus, auribus.*

For the end. A psalm for instruction, for the sons of Core.

WE HAVE heard with our ears, O God, our fathers have told us * what thou hast done in their time of old;

How thou hast driven out the heathen with thy hand, and planted them in; * how thou hast destroyed the nations and cast them out.

For they gat not the land in possession through their own sword, * neither was it their own arm that helped them;

But thy right hand, and thine arm, and the light of thy countenance; * because thou hadst a favour unto them.

Thou art my King, O God; * send help unto Jacob.

Through thee will we overthrow our enemies, * and in thy Name will we tread them under, that rise up against us.

For I will not trust in my bow, * it is not my sword that shall help me;

But it is thou that savest us from our enemies, * and puttest them to confusion that hate us.

We make our boast of God all day long, * and will praise thy Name for ever.

But now thou art far off, and puttest us to confusion, * and goest not forth with our armies.

Thou makest us to turn our backs upon our enemies, * so that they which hate us spoil our goods.

Thou lettest us be eaten up like sheep, * and hast scattered us among the heathen.

Thou sellest thy people for nought, * and takest no
    money for them.
Thou makest us to be rebuked of our
    neighbours, * to be laughed to scorn, and had in
    derision of them that are round about us.
Thou makest us to be a by-word among the
    heathen, * and that the people shake their heads
    at us.
My confusion is daily before me, * and the shame
    of my face hath covered me;
For the voice of the slanderer and blasphemer, *
    for the enemy and avenger.
And though all this be come upon us, yet do we
    not forget thee, * nor behave ourselves
    frowardly in thy covenant.
Our heart is not turned back, * neither our steps
    gone out of thy way;
No, not when thou hast smitten us into the place
    of dragons, * and covered us with the shadow
    of death.
If we have forgotten the Name of our God, and
    holden up our hands to any strange god, * shall
    not God search it out? for he knoweth the very
    secrets of the heart.

For thy sake also are we killed all the day long, *
and are counted as sheep appointed to be slain.

Up, Lord, why sleepest thou? * awake, and be not
absent from us for ever.

Wherefore hidest thou thy face, * and forgettest
our misery and trouble?

For our soul is brought low, even unto the dust; *
our belly cleaveth unto the ground.

Arise, and help us, * and deliver us for thy
mercy's sake.

Psalm 45. *Eructavit cor meum.*

*For the end. For alternate verses by the sons of
Core, for instruction. A Song concerning the
beloved.*

MY HEART is inditing of a good matter; * I speak
of the things which I have made unto the King.

My tongue is the pen * of a ready writer.

Thou art fairer than the children of men; * full of
grace are thy lips, because God hath blessed
thee for ever.

Gird thee with thy sword upon thy thigh, O thou
most Mighty, * according to thy worship and
renown.

Good luck have thou with thine honour: * ride on,
because of the word of truth, of meekness, and
righteousness; and thy right hand shall teach
thee terrible things.

Thy arrows are very sharp, and the people shall be
subdued unto thee, * even in the midst among
the King's enemies.

Thy seat, O God, endureth for ever; * the sceptre
of thy kingdom is a right sceptre.

Thou hast loved righteousness, and hated
iniquity; * wherefore God, even thy God, hath
anointed thee with the oil of gladness above thy
fellows.

All thy garments smell of myrrh, aloes, and
cassia; * out of the ivory palaces, whereby they
have made thee glad.

Kings' daughters were among thy honourable
women; * upon thy right hand did stand the
queen in a vesture of gold, wrought about with
divers colours.

Hearken, O daughter, and consider, incline thine
ear; * forget also thine own people, and thy
father's house.

So shall the King have pleasure in thy beauty; * for he is thy Lord God, and worship thou him.

And the daughter of Tyre shall be there with a gift; * like as the rich also among the people shall make their supplication before thee.

The King's daughter is all glorious within; * her clothing is of wrought gold.

She shall be brought unto the King in raiment of needle-work: * the virgins that be her fellows shall bear her company, and shall be brought unto thee.

With joy and gladness shall they be brought, * and shall enter into the King's palace.

Instead of thy fathers thou shalt have children, * whom thou mayest make princes in all lands.

I will remember thy Name from one generation to another; * therefore shall the people give thanks unto thee, world without end.

Psalm 46. *Deus noster refugium.*

For the end. For the sons of Core; a psalm concerning secret things.

GOD is our hope and strength, * a very present help in trouble.

Therefore will we not fear, though the earth be moved, * and though the hills be carried into the midst of the sea;

Though the waters thereof rage and swell, * and though the mountains shake at the tempest of the same.

The rivers of the flood thereof shall make glad the city of God; * the holy place of the tabernacle of the most Highest.

God is in the midst of her, therefore shall she not be removed; * God shall help her, and that right early.

The heathen make much ado, and the kingdoms are moved; * but God hath shewed his voice, and the earth shall melt away.

The Lord of hosts is with us; * the God of Jacob is our refuge.

O come hither, and behold the works of the
    Lord, * what destruction he hath brought upon
    the earth.
He maketh wars to cease in all the world; * he
    breaketh the bow, and knappeth the spear in
    sunder, and burneth the chariots in the fire.
Be still then, and know that I am God: * I will be
    exalted among the heathen, and I will be
    exalted in the earth.
The Lord of hosts is with us; * the God of Jacob is
    our refuge.

THE SEVENTH KATHISMA

✠ FIRST STASIS ✠

Psalm 47. *Omnes gentes, plaudite.*
For the end. A psalm for the sons of Core.

O CLAP your hands together, all ye people: * O
 sing unto God with the voice of melody.

For the Lord is high, and to be feared; * he is the
 great King upon all the earth.

He shall subdue the people under us, * and the
 nations under our feet.

He shall choose out an heritage for us, * even the
 worship of Jacob, whom he loved.

God is gone up with a merry noise, * and the Lord
 with the sound of the trump.

O sing praises, sing praises unto our God; * O
 sing praises, sing praises unto our King.

For God is the King of all the earth: * sing ye
 praises with understanding.

God reigneth over the heathen; * God sitteth upon
 his holy seat.

The princes of the people are joined unto the people of the God of Abraham; * for God, which is very high exalted, doth defend the earth, as it were with a shield.

Psalm 48. *Magnus Dominus.*

A psalm of praise for the sons of Core on the second day of the week.

GREAT is the Lord, and highly to be praised * in the city of our God, even upon his holy hill.

The hill of Sion is a fair place, and the joy of the whole earth; * upon the north-side lieth the city of the great King; God is well known in her palaces as a sure refuge.

For lo, the kings of the earth * are gathered, and gone by together.

They marvelled to see such things; * they were astonished, and suddenly cast down.

Fear came there upon them, and sorrow, * as upon a woman in her travail.

Thou shalt break the ships of the sea * through the east-wind.

Like as we have heard, so have we seen in the city
of the Lord of hosts, in the city of our God; *
God upholdeth the same for ever.
We wait for thy loving-kindness, O God, * in the
midst of thy temple.
O God, according to thy Name, so is thy praise
unto the world's end; * thy right hand is full of
righteousness.
Let the mount Sion rejoice, and the daughters of
Judah be glad, * because of thy judgements.
Walk about Sion, and go round about her; * and
tell the towers thereof.
Mark well her bulwarks, set up her houses, * that
ye may tell them that come after.
For this God is our God for ever and ever: * he
shall be our guide unto death.

Psalm 49. *Audite hæc, omnes.*
For the end. A psalm for the sons of Core.

O HEAR ye this, all ye people; * ponder it with
your ears, all ye that dwell in the world;
High and low, rich and poor, * one with another.
My mouth shall speak of wisdom, * and my heart
shall muse of understanding.

I will incline mine ear to the parable, * and shew
   my dark speech upon the harp.
Wherefore should I fear in the days of
   wickedness, * and when the wickedness of my
   heels compasseth me round about?
There be some that put their trust in their goods, *
   and boast themselves in the multitude of their
   riches.
But no man may deliver his brother, * nor make
   agreement unto God for him;
For it cost more to redeem their souls, * so that he
   must let that alone for ever;
Yea, though he live long, * and see not the grave.
For he seeth that wise men also die, and perish
   together, * as well as the ignorant and foolish,
   and leave their riches for other.
And yet they think that their houses shall continue
   for ever, and that their dwelling-places shall
   endure from one generation to another; * and
   call the lands after their own names.
Nevertheless, man will not abide in honour, *
   seeing he may be compared unto the beasts that
   perish; this is the way of them.

This is their foolishness; * and their posterity praise their saying.

They lie in the hell like sheep, death gnaweth upon them, and the righteous shall have domination over them in the morning: * their beauty shall consume in the sepulchre out of their dwelling.

But God hath delivered my soul from the place of hell; * for he shall receive me.

Be not thou afraid, though one be made rich, * or if the glory of his house be increased;

For he shall carry nothing away with him when he dieth, * neither shall his pomp follow him.

For while he lived, he counted himself an happy man; * and so long as thou doest well unto thyself, men will speak good of thee.

He shall follow the generation of his fathers, * and shall never see light.

Man being in honour hath no understanding * but is compared unto the beasts that perish.

Psalm 50. *Deus deorum.*

A psalm for Asaph.

THE Lord, even the most mighty God, hath
spoken, * and called the world, from the rising
up of the sun unto the going down thereof.

Out of Sion hath God appeared * in perfect
beauty.

Our God shall come, and shall not keep silence; *
there shall go before him a consuming fire, and
a mighty tempest shall be stirred up round
about him.

He shall call the heaven from above, * and the
earth, that he may judge his people.

Gather my saints together unto me; * those that
have made a covenant with me with sacrifice.

And the heavens shall declare his righteousness; *
for God is Judge himself.

Hear, O my people, and I will speak; * I myself
will testify against thee, O Israel; for I am God,
even thy God.

I will not reprove thee because of thy sacrifices, or for thy burnt-offerings; * because they were not alway before me.

I will take no bullock out of thine house, * nor he-goat out of thy folds.

For all the beasts of the forest are mine, * and so are the cattle upon a thousand hills.

I know all the fowls upon the mountains, * and the wild beasts of the field are in my sight.

If I be hungry, I will not tell thee; * for the whole world is mine, and all that is therein.

Thinkest thou that I will eat bulls' flesh, * and drink the blood of goats?

Offer unto God thanksgiving, * and pay thy vows unto the most Highest.

And call upon me in the time of trouble; * so will I hear thee, and thou shalt praise me.

But unto the ungodly said God, * Why dost thou preach my laws, and takest my covenant in thy mouth;

Whereas thou hatest to be reformed, * and has cast my words behind thee?

When thou sawest a thief, thou consentedst unto
 him; * and hast been partaker with the
 adulterers.
Thou hast let thy mouth speak wickedness, * and
 with thy tongue thou hast set forth deceit.
Thou satest, and spakest against thy brother; *
 yea, and hast slandered thine own mother's son.
These things hast thou done, and I held my
 tongue, and thou thoughtest wickedly, that I am
 even such a one as thyself; * but I will reprove
 thee, and set before thee the things that thou
 hast done.
O consider this, ye that forget God, * lest I pluck
 you away, and there be none to deliver you.
Whoso offereth me thanks and praise, he
 honoureth me; * and to him that ordereth his
 conversation right will I shew the salvation of
 God.

Psalm 51. *Miserere mei, Deus.*

For the end. A psalm of David, when Nathan the prophet came unto him, when he had gone in to Bathsheba.

HAVE mercy upon me, O God, after thy great goodness; * according to the multitude of thy mercies do away mine offences.

Wash me throughly from my wickedness, * and cleanse me from my sin.

For I acknowledge my faults, * and my sin is ever before me.

Against thee only have I sinned, and done this evil in thy sight; * that thou mightest be justified in thy saying, and clear when thou art judged.

Behold, I was shapen in wickedness, * and in sin hath my mother conceived me.

But lo, thou requirest truth in the inward parts, * and shalt make me to understand wisdom secretly.

Thou shalt purge me with hyssop, and I shall be clean; * thou shalt wash me, and I shall be whiter than snow.

Thou shalt make me hear of joy and gladness, *
that the bones which thou hast broken may
rejoice.

Turn thy face from my sins, * and put out all my
misdeeds.

Make me a clean heart, O God, * and renew a
right spirit within me.

Cast me not away from thy presence, * and take
not thy holy Spirit from me.

O give me the comfort of thy help again, * and
stablish me with thy free Spirit.

Then shall I teach thy ways unto the wicked, * and
sinners shall be converted unto thee.

Deliver me from blood-guiltiness, O God, thou
that art the God of my health; * and my tongue
shall sing of thy righteousness.

Thou shalt open my lips, O Lord, * and my mouth
shall shew thy praise.

For thou desirest no sacrifice, else would I give it
thee; * but thou delightest not in burnt-
offerings.

The sacrifice of God is a troubled spirit: * a
broken and contrite heart, O God, shalt thou not
despise.

O be favourable and gracious unto Sion; * build
  thou the walls of Jerusalem.
Then shalt thou be pleased with the sacrifice of
  righteousness, with the burnt-offerings and
  oblations; * then shall they offer young
  bullocks upon thine altar.

✠ THIRD STASIS ✠

Psalm 52. *Quid gloriaris?*
*For the end. A psalm of instruction by David,
when Doeg the Idumean came and told Saul that
David had gone to the house of Abimelech.*
WHY boastest thou thyself, thou tyrant, * that thou
  canst do mischief;
Whereas the goodness of God * endureth yet
  daily?
Thy tongue imagineth wickedness, * and with lies
  thou cuttest like a sharp rasor.
Thou hast loved unrighteousness more than
  goodness, * and to talk of lies more than
  righteousness.
Thou hast loved to speak all words that may do
  hurt, * O thou false tongue.

Therefore shall God destroy thee for ever; * he shall take thee, and pluck thee out of thy dwelling, and root thee out of the land of the living.

The righteous also shall see this, and fear, * and shall laugh him to scorn;

Lo, this is the man that took not God for his strength; * but trusted unto the multitude of his riches, and strengthened himself in his wickedness.

As for me, I am like a green olive-tree in the house of God; * my trust is in the tender mercy of God for ever and ever.

I will always give thanks unto thee for that thou hast done; * and I will hope in thy Name, for thy saints like it well.

Psalm 53. *Dixit insipiens.*

For the end. A psalm of David upon Maheleth, of instruction.

THE foolish body hath said in his heart, * There is no God.

Corrupt are they, and become abominable in their wickedness; * there is none that doeth good.

God looked down from heaven upon the children of men, * to see if there were any that would understand, and seek after God.

But they are all gone out of the way, they are altogether become abominable; * there is also none that doeth good, no not one.

Are not they without understanding, that work wickedness, * eating up my people as if they would eat bread? they have not called upon God.

They were afraid where no fear was; * for God hath broken the bones of him that besieged thee; thou hast put them to confusion, because God hath despised them.

O that the salvation were given unto Israel out of Sion! * O that the Lord would deliver his people out of captivity!

Then should Jacob rejoice, * and Israel should be right glad.

Psalm 54. *Deus, in nomine.*

For the end. Among the hymns of instruction by David. When the Ziphites came and said to Saul, Lo, is not David hid with us?

SAVE me, O God, for thy Name's sake, * and
    avenge me in thy strength.

Hear my prayer, O God, * and hearken unto the
    words of my mouth.

For strangers are risen up against me; * and
    tyrants, which have not God before their eyes,
    seek after my soul.

Behold, God is my helper; * the Lord is with them
    that uphold my soul.

He shall reward evil unto mine enemies: * destroy
    thou them in thy truth.

An offering of a free heart will I give thee, and
    praise thy Name, O Lord; * because it is so
    comfortable.

For he hath delivered me out of all my trouble; *
    and mine eye hath seen his desire upon mine
    enemies.

Psalm 55. *Exaudi, Deus.*

For the end. Among hymns of instruction by David.

HEAR my prayer, O God, * and hide not thyself
from my petition.

Take heed unto me, and hear me, * how I mourn
in my prayer, and am vexed.

The enemy crieth so, and the ungodly cometh on
so fast; * for they are minded to do me some
mischief; so maliciously are they set against
me.

My heart is disquieted within me, * and the fear of
death is fallen upon me.

Fearfulness and trembling are come upon me, *
and an horrible dread hath overwhelmed me.

And I said, O that I had wings like a dove! * for
then would I flee away, and be at rest.

Lo, then would I get me away far off, * and
remain in the wilderness.

I would make haste to escape, * because of the
stormy wind and tempest.

Destroy their tongues, O Lord, and divide them; *
for I have spied unrighteousness and strife in
the city.

Day and night they go about within the walls
thereof: * mischief also and sorrow are in the
midst of it.

Wickedness is therein; * deceit and guile go not
out of their streets.

For it is not an open enemy, that hath done me this
dishonour; * for then I could have borne it.

Neither was it mine adversary, that did magnify
himself against me; * for then peradventure I
would have hid myself from him.

But it was even thou, my companion, * my guide,
and mine own familiar friend.

We took sweet counsel together, * and walked in
the house of God as friends.

Let death come hastily upon them, and let them go
down quick into hell; * for wickedness is in
their dwellings, and among them.

As for me, I will call upon God, * and the Lord
shall save me.

In the evening, and morning, and at noonday will I
pray, and that instantly; * and he shall hear my
voice.

It is he that hath delivered my soul in peace from
the battle that was against me; * for there were
many with me.

Yea, even God, that endureth for ever, shall hear
me, and bring them down; * for they will not
turn, nor fear God.

He laid his hands upon such as be at peace with
him, * and he brake his covenant.

The words of his mouth were softer than butter,
having war in his heart; * his words were
smoother than oil, and yet be they very swords.

O cast thy burden upon the Lord, and he shall
nourish thee, * and shall not suffer the righteous
to fall for ever.

And as for them, * thou, O God, shalt bring them
into the pit of destruction.

The blood-thirsty and deceitful men shall not live
out half their days: * nevertheless, my trust
shall be in thee, O Lord.

THE EIGHTH KATHISMA

✠ FIRST STASIS ✠

Psalm 56. *Miserere mei, Deus.*

For the end. Concerning the people that were removed from the sanctuary. By David for a memorial, when the Philistines caught him in Gath.

BE MERCIFUL unto me, O God, for man goeth about to devour me; * he is daily fighting, and troubling me.

Mine enemies are daily in hand to swallow me up; * for they be many that fight against me, O thou most Highest.

Nevertheless, though I am sometime afraid, * yet put I my trust in thee.

I will praise God, because of his word: * I have put my trust in God, and will not fear what flesh can do unto me.

They daily mistake my words; * all that they imagine is to do me evil.

They hold all together, and keep themselves
close, * and mark my steps, when they lay wait
for my soul.
Shall they escape for their wickedness? * thou, O
God, in thy displeasure shalt cast them down.
Thou tellest my flittings; put my tears into thy
bottle: * are not these things noted in thy book?
Whensoever I call upon thee, then shall mine
enemies be put to flight: * this I know; for God
is on my side.
In God's word I will rejoice; * in the Lord's word
will I comfort me.
Yea, in God have I put my trust; * I will not be
afraid what man can do unto me.
Unto thee, O God, will I pay my vows; * unto thee
will I give thanks.
For thou hast delivered my soul from death, and
my feet from falling, * that I may walk before
God in the light of the living.

Psalm 57. *Miserere mei, Deus.*

For the end. Destroy not:
By David, for a memorial. When he fled from the
presence of Saul to the cave.

BE MERCIFUL unto me, O God, be merciful unto
me, for my soul trusteth in thee; * and under the
shadow of thy wings shall be my refuge, until
this tyranny be over-past.

I will call unto the most high God, * even unto the
God that shall perform the cause which I have
in hand.

He shall send from heaven, * and save me from
the reproof of him that would eat me up.

God shall send forth his mercy and truth: * my
soul is among lions.

And I lie even among the children of men, that are
set on fire, * whose teeth are spears and arrows,
and their tongue a sharp sword

Set up thyself, O God, above the heavens; * and
thy glory above all the earth.

They have laid a net for my feet, and pressed
down my soul; * they have digged a pit before
me, and are fallen into the midst of it
themselves.

My heart is fixed, O God, my heart is fixed; * I
will sing, and give praise.

Awake up, my glory; awake, lute and harp: * I
myself will awake right early.

I will give thanks unto thee, O Lord, among the
people; * and I will sing unto thee among the
nations.

For the greatness of thy mercy reacheth unto the
heavens, * and thy truth unto the clouds.

Set up thyself, O God, above the heavens; * and
thy glory above all the earth.

Psalm 58. *Si vere utique.*

For the end. Destroy not:
by David, for a memorial.

ARE your minds set upon righteousness, O ye
congregation? * and do ye judge the thing that
is right, O ye sons of men?

Yea, ye imagine mischief in your heart upon the
earth, * and your hands deal with wickedness.

The ungodly are froward, even from their
mother's womb; * as soon as they are born,
they go astray, and speak lies.

They are as venomous as the poison of a
    serpent, * even like the deaf adder that stoppeth
    her ears;
Which refuseth to hear the voice of the charmer, *
    charm he never so wisely.
Break their teeth, O God, in their mouths; smite
    the jaw-bones of the lions, O Lord: * let them
    fall away like water that runneth apace; and
    when they shoot their arrows let them be rooted
    out.
Let them consume away like a snail, and be like
    the untimely fruit of a woman; * and let them
    not see the sun.
Or ever your pots be made hot with thorns, * so
    let indignation vex him, even as a thing that is
    raw.
The righteous shall rejoice when he seeth the
    vengeance; * he shall wash his footsteps in the
    blood of the ungodly.
So that a man shall say, Verily there is a reward
    for the righteous; * doubtless there is a God that
    judgeth the earth.

Psalm 59. *Eripe me de inimicis.*
For the end. Destroy not:
By David for a memorial, when Saul sent and watched his house to kill him.

DELIVER me from mine enemies, O God; * defend me from them that rise up against me.

O deliver me from the wicked doers, * and save me from the blood-thirsty men.

For lo, they lie waiting for my soul; * the mighty men are gathered against me, without any offence or fault of me, O Lord.

They run and prepare themselves without my fault; * arise thou therefore to help me, and behold.

Stand up, O Lord God of hosts, thou God of Israel, to visit all the heathen, * and be not merciful unto them that offend of malicious wickedness.

They go to and fro in the evening, * they grin like a dog, and run about through the city.

Behold, they speak with their mouth, and swords are in their lips; * for who doth hear?

But thou, O Lord, shalt have them in derision, *
and thou shalt laugh all the heathen to scorn.

My strength will I ascribe unto thee; * for thou art
the God of my refuge.

God sheweth me his goodness plenteously; * and
God shall let me see my desire upon mine
enemies.

Slay them not, lest my people forget it; * but
scatter them abroad among the people, and put
them down, O Lord, our defence.

For the sin of their mouth, and for the words of
their lips, they shall be taken in their pride: *
and why? their preaching is of cursing and lies.

Consume them in thy wrath, consume them, that
they may perish; * and know that it is God that
ruleth in Jacob, and unto the ends of the world.

And in the evening they will return, * grin like a
dog, and will go about the city.

They will run here and there for meat, * and
grudge if they be not satisfied.

As for me, I will sing of thy power, and will praise
thy mercy betimes in the morning; * for thou
hast been my defence and refuge in the day of
my trouble.

Unto thee, O my strength, will I sing; * for thou, O God, art my refuge, and my merciful God.

Psalm 60. *Deus, repulisti nos.*

For the end. For them that shall yet be changed. For an inscription by David for instruction. When he had burned Aram-naharaim of Syria, and Aram-zobah, and Joab had returned and smitten twelve thousand in the Valley of Salt.

O GOD, thou hast cast us out, and scattered us abroad; * thou hast also been displeased; O turn thee unto us again.

Thou hast moved the land, and divided it: * heal the sores thereof, for it shaketh.

Thou hast shewed thy people heavy things; * thou hast given us a drink of deadly wine.

Thou hast given a token for such as fear thee, * that they may triumph because of the truth.

Therefore were thy beloved delivered: * help me with thy right hand, and hear me.

God hath spoken in his holiness, I will rejoice, and divide Sichem, * and mete out the valley of Succoth.

Gilead is mine, and Manasses is mine; * Ephraim also is the strength of my head; Judah is my law-giver;

Moab is my wash-pot; over Edom will I cast out my shoe; * Philistia, be thou glad of me.

Who will lead me into the strong city? * who will bring me into Edom?

Hast not thou cast us out, O God? * wilt not thou, O God, go out with our hosts?

O be thou our help in trouble; * for vain is the help of man.

Through God will we do great acts; * for it is he that shall tread down our enemies.

Psalm 61. *Exaudi, Deus.*

For the end. Among the hymns of David.

HEAR my crying, O God, * give ear unto my
    prayer.

From the ends of the earth will I call upon thee, *
    when my heart is in heaviness.

O set me up upon the rock that is higher than I; *
    for thou hast been my hope, and a strong tower
    for me against the enemy.

I will dwell in thy tabernacle for ever, * and my
    trust shall be under the covering of thy wings.

For thou, O Lord, hast heard my desires, * and
    hast given an heritage unto those that fear thy
    Name.

Thou shalt grant the King a long life, * that his
    years may endure throughout all generations.

He shall dwell before God for ever: * O prepare
    thy loving mercy and faithfulness, that they
    may preserve him.

So will I always sing praise unto thy Name, * that
    I may daily perform my vows.

✠ THIRD STASIS ✠

Psalm 62. *Nonne Deo?*

For the end. A psalm of David for Idithun.

MY SOUL truly waiteth still upon God; * for of him cometh my salvation.

He verily is my strength and my salvation; * he is my defence, so that I shall not greatly fall.

How long will ye imagine mischief against every man? * ye shall be slain all the sort of you; yea, as a tottering wall shall ye be, and like a broken hedge.

Their device is only how to put him out whom God will exalt; * their delight is in lies; they give good words with their mouth, but curse with their heart.

Nevertheless, my soul, wait thou still upon God; * for my hope is in him.

He truly is my strength and my salvation; * he is my defence, so that I shall not fall.

In God is my health, and my glory; * the rock of my might, and in God is my trust.

O put your trust in him alway, ye people; * pour out your hearts before him, for God is our hope.

As for the children of men, they are but vanity; *
the children of men are deceitful upon the
weights, they are altogether lighter than vanity
itself.

O trust not in wrong and robbery, give not
yourselves unto vanity: * if riches increase, set
not your heart upon them.

God spake once, and twice I have also heard the
same, * that power belongeth unto God;

And that thou, Lord, art merciful; * for thou
rewardest every man according to his work.

Psalm 63. *Deus, Deus meus.*

*A psalm of David. When he was in the wilderness
of Idumea.*

O GOD, thou art my God; * early will I seek thee.

My soul thirsteth for thee, my flesh also longeth
after thee, * in a barren and dry land where no
water is.

Thus have I looked for thee in holiness, * that I
might behold thy power and glory.

For thy loving-kindness is better than the life
itself: * my lips shall praise thee.

As long as I live will I magnify thee on this
    manner, * and lift up my hands in thy Name.
My soul shall be satisfied, even as it were with
    marrow and fatness, * when my mouth praiseth
    thee with joyful lips.
Have I not remembered thee in my bed, * and
    thought upon thee when I was waking?
Because thou hast been my helper; * therefore
    under the shadow of thy wings will I rejoice.
My soul hangeth upon thee; * thy right hand hath
    upholden me.
These also that seek the hurt of my soul, * they
    shall go under the earth.
Let them fall upon the edge of the sword, * that
    they may be a portion for foxes.
But the King shall rejoice in God; all they also
    that swear by him shall be commended; * for
    the mouth of them that speak lies shall be
    stopped.

Psalm 64. *Exaudi, Deus.*
For the end. A psalm of David.
HEAR my voice, O God, in my prayer; * preserve
    my life from fear of the enemy.

Hide me from the gathering together of the froward, * and from the insurrection of wicked doers;

Who have whet their tongue like a sword, * and shoot out their arrows, even bitter words;

That they may privily shoot at him that is perfect: * suddenly do they hit him, and fear not.

They encourage themselves in mischief, * and commune among themselves how they may lay snares, and say that no man shall see them.

They imagine wickedness, and practise it; * that they keep secret among themselves, every man in the deep of his heart.

But God shall suddenly shoot at them with a swift arrow, * that they shall be wounded.

Yea, their own tongues shall make them fall; * insomuch that whoso seeth them shall laugh them to scorn.

And all men that see it shall say, This hath God done; * for they shall perceive that it is his work.

The righteous shall rejoice in the Lord, and put his trust in him; * and all they that are true of heart shall be glad.

THE NINTH KATHISMA

✠ FIRST STASIS ✠

Psalm 65. *Te decet hymnus.*

For the end. A psalm and song of David.

THOU, O God, art praised in Sion; * and unto thee
   shall the vow be performed in Jerusalem.

Thou that hearest the prayer, * unto thee shall all
   flesh come.

My misdeeds prevail against me: * O be thou
   merciful unto our sins.

Blessed is the man whom thou choosest, and
   receivest unto thee: * he shall dwell in thy
   court, and shall be satisfied with the pleasures
   of thy house, even of thy holy temple.

Thou shalt shew us wonderful things in thy
   righteousness, O God of our salvation; * thou
   that art the hope of all the ends of the earth, and
   of them that remain in the broad sea.

Who in his strength setteth fast the mountains, *
   and is girded about with power.

Who stilleth the raging of the sea, * and the noise
of his waves, and the madness of the people.

They also that dwell in the uttermost parts of the
earth shall be afraid at thy tokens, * thou that
makest the outgoings of the morning and
evening to praise thee.

Thou visitest the earth, and blessest it; * thou
makest it very plenteous.

The river of God is full of water: * thou preparest
their corn, for so thou providest for the earth.

Thou waterest her furrows, thou sendest rain into
the little valleys thereof; * thou makest it soft
with the drops of rain, and blessest the increase
of it.

Thou crownest the year with thy goodness; * and
thy clouds drop fatness.

They shall drop upon the dwellings of the
wilderness; * and the little hills shall rejoice on
every side.

The folds shall be full of sheep; * the valleys also
shall stand so thick with corn, that they shall
laugh and sing.

Psalm 66. *Jubilate Deo.*

For the end. A song of a psalm of resurrection.

O BE joyful in God, all ye lands; * sing praises
    unto the honour of his Name, make his praise to
    be glorious.

Say unto God, O how wonderful art thou in thy
    works! * through the greatness of thy power
    shall thine enemies be found liars unto thee.

For all the world shall worship thee, * sing of
    thee, and praise thy Name.

O come hither, and behold the works of God; *
    how wonderful he is in his doing toward the
    children of men.

He turned the sea into dry land, * so that they
    went through the water on foot; there did we
    rejoice thereof.

He ruleth with his power for ever; his eyes behold
    the people: * and such as will not believe shall
    not be able to exalt themselves.

O praise our God, ye people, * and make the voice
    of his praise to be heard;

Who holdeth our soul in life; * and suffereth not
    our feet to slip.

For thou, O God, hast proved us; * thou also hast
tried us, like as silver is tried.

Thou broughtest us into the snare; * and laidest
trouble upon our loins.

Thou sufferedst men to ride over our heads; * we
went through fire and water, and thou
broughtest us out into a wealthy place.

I will go into thine house with burnt-offerings, *
and will pay thee my vows, which I promised
with my lips, and spake with my mouth, when I
was in trouble.

I will offer unto thee fat burnt-sacrifices, with the
incense of rams; * I will offer bullocks and
goats.

O come hither, and hearken, all ye that fear
God; * and I will tell you what he hath done for
my soul.

I called unto him with my mouth, * and gave him
praises with my tongue.

If I incline unto wickedness with mine heart, * the
Lord will not hear me.

But God hath heard me; * and considered the
voice of my prayer.

Praised be God, who hath not cast out my
  prayer, * nor turned his mercy from me.

Psalm 67. *Deus misereatur.*

For the end. A psalm of David among the hymns.

GOD be merciful unto us, and bless us, * and shew
  us the light of his countenance, and be merciful
  unto us:

That thy way may be known upon earth, * thy
  saving health among all nations.

Let the people praise thee, O God; * yea, let all
  the people praise thee.

O let the nations rejoice and be glad; * for thou
  shalt judge the folk righteously, and govern the
  nations upon earth.

Let the people praise thee, O God; * let all the
  people praise thee.

Then shall the earth bring forth her increase; * and
  God, even our own God, shall give us his
  blessing.

God shall bless us; * and all the ends of the world
  shall fear him.

Psalm 68. *Exurgat Deus.*

For the end. A psalm of a song of David.

LET God arise, and let his enemies be scattered: *
let them also that hate him flee before him.

Like as the smoke vanisheth, so shalt thou drive
them away; * and like as wax melteth at the
fire, so let the ungodly perish at the presence of
God.

But let the righteous be glad and rejoice before
God; * let them also be merry and joyful.

O sing unto God, and sing praises unto his
Name, * magnify him that rideth upon the
heavens, as it were upon an horse; praise him in
his Name יהוה, and rejoice before him.

He is a father of the fatherless, and defendeth the
cause of the widows; * even God in his holy
habitation.

He is the God that maketh men to be of one mind
in an house, and bringeth the prisoners out of
captivity; * but letteth the runagates continue in
scarceness.

O God, when thou wentest forth before the people; * when thou wentest through the wilderness;

The earth shook, and the heavens dropped at the presence of God; * even as Sinai also was moved at the presence of God, who is the God of Israel.

Thou, O God, sentest a gracious rain upon thine inheritance, * and refreshedst it when it was weary.

Thy congregation shall dwell therein; * for thou, O God, hast of thy goodness prepared for the poor.

The Lord gave the word; * great was the company of the preachers.

Kings with their armies did flee, and were discomfited, * and they of the household divided the spoil.

Though ye have lien among the pots, yet shall ye be as the wings of a dove * that is covered with silver wings, and her feathers like gold.

When the Almighty scattered kings for their sake, * then were they as white as snow in Salmon.

As the hill of Basan, so is God's hill; * even an
high hill, as the hill of Basan.

Why hop ye so, ye high hills? this is God's hill, in
the which it pleaseth him to dwell; * yea, the
Lord will abide in it for ever.

The chariots of God are twenty thousand, even
thousands of angels; * and the Lord is among
them, as in the holy place of Sinai.

Thou art gone up on high, thou hast led captivity
captive, and received gifts for men; * yea, even
for thine enemies, that the Lord God might
dwell among them.

Praised be the Lord daily, * even the God who
helpeth us, and poureth his benefits upon us.

He is our God, even the God of whom cometh
salvation: * God is the Lord, by whom we
escape death.

God shall wound the head of his enemies, * and
the hairy scalp of such a one as goeth on still in
his wickedness.

The Lord hath said, I will bring my people again,
as I did from Basan; * mine own will I bring
again, as I did sometime from the deep of the
sea.

That thy foot may be dipped in the blood of thine
   enemies, * and that the tongue of thy dogs may
   be red through the same.
It is well seen, O God, how thou goest; * how
   thou, my God and King, goest in the sanctuary.
The singers go before, the minstrels follow after, *
   in the midst are the damsels playing with the
   timbrels.
Give thanks, O Israel, unto God the Lord in the
   congregations, * from the ground of the heart.
There is little Benjamin their ruler, and the princes
   of Judah their counsel; * the princes of
   Zabulon, and the princes of Nephthali.
Thy God hath sent forth strength for thee; *
   stablish the thing, O God, that thou hast
   wrought in us,
For thy temple's sake at Jerusalem; * so shall
   kings bring presents unto thee.
When the company of the spear-men, and
   multitude of the mighty are scattered abroad
   among the beasts of the people, so that they
   humbly bring pieces of silver; * and when he
   hath scattered the people that delight in war;

Then shall the princes come out of Egypt; * the
    Morians' land shall soon stretch out her hands
    unto God.
Sing unto God, O ye kingdoms of the earth; * O
    sing praises unto the Lord;
Who sitteth in the heavens over all from the
    beginning: * lo, he doth send out his voice, yea,
    and that a mighty voice.
Ascribe ye the power to God over Israel; * his
    worship and strength is in the clouds.
O God, wonderful art thou in thy holy places: *
    even the God of Israel, he will give strength and
    power unto his people; blessed be God.

✠ THIRD STASIS ✠

Psalm 69. *Salvum me fac.*

For the end. A psalm of David for alternate verses.

SAVE me, O God; * for the waters are come in, even unto my soul.

I stick fast in the deep mire, where no ground is; * I am come into deep waters, so that the floods run over me.

I am weary of crying; my throat is dry; * my sight faileth me for waiting so long upon my God.

They that hate me without a cause are more than the hairs of my head; * they that are mine enemies, and would destroy me guiltless, are mighty.

I paid them the things that I never took: * God, thou knowest my simpleness, and my faults are not hid from thee.

Let not them that trust in thee, O Lord God of hosts, be ashamed for my cause; * let not those that seek thee be confounded through me, O Lord God of Israel.

And why? for thy sake have I suffered reproof; *
shame hath covered my face.

I am become a stranger unto my brethren, * even
an alien unto my mother's children.

For the zeal of thine house hath even eaten me; *
and the rebukes of them that rebuked thee are
fallen upon me.

I wept, and chastened myself with fasting, * and
that was turned to my reproof.

I put on sackcloth also, * and they jested upon me.

They that sit in the gate speak against me, * and
the drunkards make songs upon me.

But, Lord, I make my prayer unto thee * in an
acceptable time.

Hear me, O God, in the multitude of thy mercy, *
even in the truth of thy salvation.

Take me out of the mire, that I sink not; * O let
me be delivered from them that hate me, and
out of the deep waters.

Let not the water-flood drown me, neither let the
deep swallow me up; * and let not the pit shut
her mouth upon me.

Hear me, O Lord, for thy loving-kindness is comfortable; * turn thee unto me according to the multitude of thy mercies.

And hide not thy face from thy servant, for I am in trouble: * O haste thee, and hear me.

Draw nigh unto my soul, and save it; * O deliver me, because of mine enemies.

Thou hast known my reproof, my shame, and my dishonour: * mine adversaries are all in thy sight.

Thy rebuke hath broken my heart; I am full of heaviness: * I looked for some to have pity on me, but there was no man, neither found I any to comfort me.

They gave me gall to eat; * and when I was thirsty they gave me vinegar to drink.

Let their table be made a snare to take themselves withal; * and let the things that should have been for their wealth be unto them an occasion of falling.

Let their eyes be blinded, that they see not; * and ever bow thou down their backs.

Pour out thine indignation upon them, * and let thy wrathful displeasure take hold of them.

Let their habitation be void, * and no man to dwell
in their tents.

For they persecute him whom thou hast smitten; *
and they talk how they may vex them whom
thou hast wounded.

Let them fall from one wickedness to another, *
and not come into thy righteousness.

Let them be wiped out of the book of the living, *
and not be written among the righteous.

As for me, when I am poor and in heaviness, * thy
help, O God, shall lift me up.

I will praise the Name of God with a song, * and
magnify it with thanksgiving.

This also shall please the Lord * better than a
bullock that hath horns and hoofs.

The humble shall consider this, and be glad: *
seek ye after God, and your soul shall live.

For the Lord heareth the poor, * and despiseth not
his prisoners.

Let heaven and earth praise him: * the sea, and all
that moveth therein.

For God will save Sion, and build the cities of
Judah, * that men may dwell there, and have it
in possession.

The posterity also of his servants shall inherit it; *
and they that love his Name shall dwell therein.

Psalm 70. *Deus, in adjutorium.*

*For the end. By David for a remembrance; that
the Lord may save me.*

HASTE thee, O God, to deliver me; * make haste
to help me, O Lord.

Let them be ashamed and confounded that seek
after my soul; * let them be turned backward
and put to confusion that wish me evil.

Let them for their reward be soon brought to
shame, * that cry over me, There, there.

But let all those that seek thee be joyful and glad
in thee: * and let all such as delight in thy
salvation say alway, The Lord be praised.

As for me, I am poor and in misery: * haste thee
unto me, O God.

Thou art my helper and my redeemer: * O Lord,
make no long tarrying.

THE TENTH KATHISMA

✠ FIRST STASIS ✠

Psalm 71. *In te, Domine, speravi.*

*By David. A psalm sung by the sons of Jonadab
and the first that were taken captive.*

IN THEE, O Lord, have I put my trust, let me never
be put to confusion, * but rid me and deliver me
in thy righteousness, incline thine ear unto me,
and save me.

Be thou my strong hold, whereunto I may alway
resort: * thou hast promised to help me, for
thou art my house of defence and my castle.

Deliver me, O my God, out of the hand of the
ungodly, * out of the hand of the unrighteous
and cruel man.

For thou, O Lord God, art the thing that I long
for: * thou art my hope, even from my youth.

Through thee have I been holden up ever since I
was born: * thou art he that took me out of my
mother's womb; my praise shall be always of
thee.

I am become as it were a monster unto many, *
but my sure trust is in thee.
O let my mouth be filled with thy praise, * that I
may sing of thy glory and honour all the day
long.
Cast me not away in the time of age; * forsake me
not when my strength faileth me.
For mine enemies speak against me, and they that
lay wait for my soul take their counsel together,
saying, * God hath forsaken him; persecute
him, and take him, for there is none to deliver
him.
Go not far from me, O God; * my God, haste thee
to help me.
Let them be confounded and perish that are
against my soul; * let them be covered with
shame and dishonour that seek to do me evil.
As for me, I will patiently abide always, * and
will praise thee more and more.
My mouth shall daily speak of thy righteousness
and salvation; * for I know no end thereof.
I will go forth in the strength of the Lord God, *
and will make mention of thy righteousness
only.

Thou, O God, hast taught me from my youth up until now; * therefore will I tell of thy wondrous works.

Forsake me not, O God, in mine old age, when I am gray-headed, * until I have shewed thy strength unto this generation, and thy power to all them that are yet for to come.

Thy righteousness, O God, is very high, * and great things are they that thou hast done; O God, who is like unto thee?

O what great troubles and adversities hast thou shewed me, and yet didst thou turn and refresh me; * yea, and broughtest me from the deep of the earth again.

Thou hast brought me to great honour, * and comforted me on every side.

Therefore will I praise thee and thy faithfulness, O God, playing upon an instrument of musick: * unto thee will I sing upon the harp, O thou Holy One of Israel.

My lips will be fain when I sing unto thee; * and so will my soul whom thou hast delivered.

My tongue also shall talk of thy righteousness all
the day long; * for they are confounded and
brought unto shame that seek to do me evil.

Psalm 72. *Deus, judicium.*

For Solomon.

GIVE the King thy judgements, O God, * and thy
righteousness unto the King's son.

Then shall he judge thy people according unto
right, * and defend the poor.

The mountains also shall bring peace, * and the
little hills righteousness unto the people.

He shall keep the simple folk by their right, *
defend the children of the poor, and punish the
wrong-doer.

They shall fear thee, as long as the sun and moon
endureth, * from one generation to another.

He shall come down like the rain into a fleece of
wool, * even as the drops that water the earth.

In his time shall the righteous flourish; * yea, and
abundance of peace, so long as the moon
endureth.

His dominion shall be also from the one sea to the other, * and from the flood unto the world's end.

They that dwell in the wilderness shall kneel before him; * his enemies shall lick the dust.

The kings of Tharsis and of the isles shall give presents; * the kings of Arabia and Saba shall bring gifts.

All kings shall fall down before him; * all nations shall do him service.

For he shall deliver the poor when he crieth; * the needy also, and him that hath no helper.

He shall be favourable to the simple and needy, * and shall preserve the souls of the poor.

He shall deliver their souls from falsehood and wrong; * and dear shall their blood be in his sight.

He shall live, and unto him shall be given of the gold of Arabia; * prayer shall be made ever unto him, and daily shall he be praised.

There shall be an heap of corn in the earth, high upon the hills; * his fruit shall shake like Libanus, and shall be green in the city like grass upon the earth.

His Name shall endure for ever; his Name shall
  remain under the sun among the posterities, *
  which shall be blessed through him; and all the
  heathen shall praise him.
Blessed be the Lord God, even the God of
  Israel, * which only doeth wondrous things;
And blessed be the Name of his majesty for
  ever: * and all the earth shall be filled with his
  majesty. Amen, Amen.

✠ SECOND STASIS ✠

Psalm 73. *Quam bonus Israël!*
A psalm for Asaph.

TRULY God is loving unto Israel: * even unto such
  as are of a clean heart.
Nevertheless, my feet were almost gone, * my
  treadings had well-nigh slipt.
And why? I was grieved at the wicked: * I do also
  see the ungodly in such prosperity.
For they are in no peril of death; * but are lusty
  and strong.
They come in no misfortune like other folk; *
  neither are they plagued like other men.

And this is the cause that they are so holden with
    pride, * and overwhelmed with cruelty.
Their eyes swell with fatness, * and they do even
    what they lust.
They corrupt other, and speak of wicked
    blasphemy; * their talking is against the most
    High.
For they stretch forth their mouth unto the heaven,
    * and their tongue goeth through the world.
Therefore fall the people unto them, * and
    thereout suck they no small advantage.
Tush, say they, how should God perceive it? * is
    there knowledge in the most High?
Lo, these are the ungodly, these prosper in the
    world, and these have riches in possession: *
    and I said, Then have I cleansed my heart in
    vain, and washed mine hands in innocency.
All the day long have I been punished, * and
    chastened every morning.
Yea, and I had almost said even as they; * but lo,
    then I should have condemned the generation of
    thy children.
Then thought I to understand this; * but it was too
    hard for me,

Until I went into the sanctuary of God: * then understood I the end of these men;

Namely, how thou dost set them in slippery places, * and castest them down, and destroyest them.

O how suddenly do they consume, * perish, and come to a fearful end!

Yea, even like as a dream when one awaketh; * so shalt thou make their image to vanish out of the city.

Thus my heart was grieved, * and it went even through my reins.

So foolish was I, and ignorant, * even as it were a beast before thee.

Nevertheless, I am alway by thee; * for thou hast holden me by my right hand.

Thou shalt guide me with thy counsel, * and after that receive me with glory.

Whom have I in heaven but thee? * and there is none upon earth that I desire in comparison of thee.

My flesh and my heart faileth; * but God is the strength of my heart, and my portion for ever.

For lo, they that forsake thee shall perish; * thou hast destroyed all them that commit fornication against thee.

But it is good for me to hold me fast by God, to put my trust in the Lord God, * and to speak of all thy works in the gates of the daughter of Sion.

Psalm 74. *Ut quid, Deus?*
A psalm of instruction for Asaph.

O GOD, wherefore art thou absent from us so long? * why is thy wrath so hot against the sheep of thy pasture?

O think upon thy congregation, * whom thou hast purchased and redeemed of old.

Think upon the tribe of thine inheritance, * and mount Sion, wherein thou hast dwelt.

Lift up thy feet, that thou mayest utterly destroy every enemy, * which hath done evil in thy sanctuary.

Thine adversaries roar in the midst of thy congregations, * and set up their banners for tokens.

He that hewed timber afore out of the thick trees, * was known to bring it to an excellent work.

But now they break down all the carved work thereof * with axes and hammers.

They have set fire upon thy holy places, * and have defiled the dwelling-place of thy Name, even unto the ground.

Yea, they said in their hearts, Let us make havock of them altogether: * thus have they burnt up all the houses of God in the land.

We see not our tokens, there is not one prophet more; * no, not one is there among us, that understandeth any more.

O God, how long shall the adversary do this dishonour? * how long shall the enemy blaspheme thy Name, for ever?

Why withdrawest thou thy hand? * why pluckest thou not thy right hand out of thy bosom to consume the enemy?

For God is my King of old; * the help that is done upon earth he doeth it himself.

Thou didst divide the sea through thy power; * thou brakest the heads of the dragons in the waters.

Thou smotest the heads of Leviathan in pieces, *
and gavest him to be meat for the people in the
wilderness.

Thou broughtest out fountains and waters out of
the hard rocks; * thou driedst up mighty waters.

The day is thine, and the night is thine; * thou hast
prepared the light and the sun.

Thou hast set all the borders of the earth; * thou
hast made summer and winter.

Remember this, O Lord, how the enemy hath
rebuked; * and how the foolish people hath
blasphemed thy Name.

O deliver not the soul of thy turtle-dove unto the
multitude of the enemies; * and forget not the
congregation of the poor for ever.

Look upon the covenant; * for all the earth is full
of darkness and cruel habitations.

O let not the simple go away ashamed; * but let
the poor and needy give praise unto thy Name.

Arise, O God, maintain thine own cause; *
remember how the foolish man blasphemeth
thee daily.

Forget not the voice of thine enemies: * the presumption of them that hate thee increaseth ever more and more.

✠ THIRD STASIS ✠

Psalm 75. *Confitebimur tibi.*
For the end. Destroy not:
A psalm of a song for Asaph.

UNTO thee, O God, do we give thanks; * yea, unto thee do we give thanks.

Thy Name also is so nigh; * and that do thy wondrous works declare.

When I receive the congregation, * I shall judge according unto right.

The earth is weak, and all the inhabiters thereof: * I bear up the pillars of it.

I said unto the fools, Deal not so madly; * and to the ungodly, Set not up your horn.

Set not up your horn on high, * and speak not with a stiff neck.

For promotion cometh neither from the east, nor from the west, * nor yet from the south.

And why? God is the Judge; * he putteth down
    one, and setteth up another.

For in the hand of the Lord there is a cup, and the
    wine is red; * it is full mixed, and he poureth
    out of the same.

As for the dregs thereof, * all the ungodly of the
    earth shall drink them, and suck them out.

But I will talk of the God of Jacob, * and praise
    him for ever.

All the horns of the ungodly also will I break, *
    and the horns of the righteous shall be exalted.

Psalm 76. *Notus in Judæa.*

*For the end. Among the hymns, a psalm for
Asaph:
A song for the Assyrian.*

IN JEWRY is God known; * his Name is great in
    Israel.

At Salem is his tabernacle, * and his dwelling in
    Sion.

There brake he the arrows of the bow, * the
    shield, the sword, and the battle.

Thou art of more honour and might * than the
    hills of the robbers.

The proud are robbed, they have slept their
sleep; * and all the men whose hands were
mighty have found nothing.
At thy rebuke, O God of Jacob, * both the chariot
and horse are fallen.
Thou, even thou art to be feared; * and who may
stand in thy sight when thou art angry?
Thou didst cause thy judgement to be heard from
heaven; * the earth trembled, and was still;
When God arose to judgement, * and to help all
the meek upon earth.
The fierceness of man shall turn to thy praise; *
and the fierceness of them shalt thou refrain.
Promise unto the Lord your God, and keep it, all
ye that are round about him; * bring presents
unto him that ought to be feared.
He shall refrain the spirit of princes, * and is
wonderful among the kings of the earth.

Psalm 77. *Voce mea ad Dominum.*
For the end. For Idithun, a psalm of Asaph.
I WILL cry unto God with my voice; * even unto
God will I cry with my voice, and he shall
hearken unto me.

In the time of my trouble I sought the Lord: * my sore ran and ceased not in the night-season; my soul refused comfort.

When I am in heaviness, I will think upon God; * when my heart is vexed, I will complain.

Thou holdest mine eyes waking: * I am so feeble, that I cannot speak.

I have considered the days of old, * and the years that are past.

I call to remembrance my song, * and in the night I commune with mine own heart, and search out my spirits.

Will the Lord absent himself for ever? * and will he be no more intreated?

Is his mercy clean gone for ever? * and is his promise come utterly to an end for evermore?

Hath God forgotten to be gracious? * and will he shut up his loving-kindness in displeasure?

And I said, It is mine own infirmity; * but I will remember the years of the right hand of the most Highest.

I will remember the works of the Lord, * and call to mind thy wonders of old time.

I will think also of all thy works, * and my talking
shall be of thy doings.

Thy way, O God, is holy: * who is so great a God
as our God?

Thou art the God that doeth wonders, * and hast
declared thy power among the people.

Thou hast mightily delivered thy people, * even
the sons of Jacob and Joseph.

The waters saw thee, O God, the waters saw thee,
and were afraid; * the depths also were
troubled.

The clouds poured out water, the air thundered, *
and thine arrows went abroad.

The voice of thy thunder was heard round about: *
the lightnings shone upon the ground; the earth
was moved, and shook withal.

Thy way is in the sea, and thy paths in the great
waters, * and thy footsteps are not known.

Thou leddest thy people like sheep, * by the hand
of Moses and Aaron.

THE ELEVENTH KATHISMA

✠ FIRST STASIS ✠

Psalm 78. *Attendite, popule.*

A psalm of instruction for Asaph.

HEAR my law, O my people; * incline your ears
 unto the words of my mouth.

I will open my mouth in a parable; * I will declare
 hard sentences of old;

Which we have heard and known, * and such as
 our fathers have told us;

That we should not hide them from the children of
 the generations to come; * but to shew the
 honour of the Lord, his mighty and wonderful
 works that he hath done.

He made a covenant with Jacob, and gave Israel a
 law, * which he commanded our forefathers to
 teach their children;

That their posterity might know it, * and the
 children which were yet unborn;

To the intent that when they came up, * they
 might shew their children the same;

That they might put their trust in God; * and not to forget the works of God, but to keep his commandments;

And not to be as their forefathers, a faithless and stubborn generation; * a generation that set not their heart aright, and whose spirit cleaveth not stedfastly unto God;

Like as the children of Ephraim; * who being harnessed, and carrying bows, turned themselves back in the day of battle.

They kept not the covenant of God, * and would not walk in his law;

But forgat what he had done, * and the wonderful works that he had shewed for them.

Marvellous things did he in the sight of our forefathers, in the land of Egypt, * even in the field of Zoan.

He divided the sea, and let them go through; * he made the waters to stand on an heap.

In the day-time also he led them with a cloud, * and all the night through with a light of fire.

He clave the hard rocks in the wilderness, * and gave them drink thereof, as it had been out of the great depth.

He brought waters out of the stony rock, * so that it gushed out like the rivers.

Yet for all this they sinned more against him, * and provoked the most Highest in the wilderness.

They tempted God in their hearts, * and required meat for their lust.

They spake against God also, saying, * Shall God prepare a table in the wilderness?

He smote the stony rock indeed, that the waters gushed out, and the streams flowed withal; * but can he give bread also, or provide flesh for his people?

When the Lord heard this, he was wroth; * so the fire was kindled in Jacob, and there came up heavy displeasure against Israel;

Because they believed not in God, * and put not their trust in his help.

So he commanded the clouds above, * and opened the doors of heaven.

He rained down manna also upon them for to eat, * and gave them food from heaven.

So man did eat angels' food; * for he sent them meat enough.

He caused the east-wind to blow under heaven; *
and through his power he brought in the south-
west-wind.

He rained flesh upon them as thick as dust, * and
feathered fowls like as the sand of the sea.

He let it fall among their tents, * even round about
their habitation.

So they did eat and were well filled, for he gave
them their own desire: * they were not
disappointed of their lust.

But while the meat was yet in their mouths, the
heavy wrath of God came upon them, and slew
the wealthiest of them; * yea, and smote down
the chosen men that were in Israel.

But for all this they sinned yet more, * and
believed not his wondrous works.

Therefore their days did he consume in vanity, *
and their years in trouble.

When he slew them, they sought him, * and
turned them early, and inquired after God.

And they remembered that God was their
strength, * and that the high God was their
redeemer.

Nevertheless, they did but flatter him with their mouth, * and dissembled with him in their tongue.

For their heart was not whole with him, * neither continued they stedfast in his covenant.

But he was so merciful, that he forgave their misdeeds, * and destroyed them not.

Yea, many a time turned he his wrath away, * and would not suffer his whole displeasure to arise.

For he considered that they were but flesh, * and that they were even a wind that passeth away, and cometh not again.

Many a time did they provoke him in the wilderness, * and grieved him in the desert.

They turned back, and tempted God, * and moved the Holy One in Israel.

They thought not of his hand, * and of the day when he delivered them from the hand of the enemy;

How he had wrought his miracles in Egypt, * and his wonders in the field of Zoan.

He turned their waters into blood, * so that they might not drink of the rivers.

He sent lice among them, and devoured them
up; * and frogs to destroy them.

He gave their fruit unto the caterpillar, * and their
labour unto the grasshopper.

He destroyed their vines with hail-stones, * and
their mulberry-trees with the frost.

He smote their cattle also with hail-stones, * and
their flocks with hot thunderbolts.

He cast upon them the furiousness of his wrath,
anger, displeasure and trouble: * and sent evil
angels among them.

He made a way to his indignation, and spared not
their soul from death; * but gave their life over
to the pestilence;

And smote all the first-born in Egypt, * the most
principal and mightiest in the dwellings of
Ham.

But as for his own people, he led them forth like
sheep, * and carried them in the wilderness like
a flock.

He brought them out safely, that they should not
fear, * and overwhelmed their enemies with the
sea.

And brought them within the borders of his
    sanctuary, * even to his mountain which he
    purchased with his right hand.
He cast out the heathen also before them, * caused
    their land to be divided among them for an
    heritage, and made the tribes of Israel to dwell
    in their tents.
So they tempted and displeased the most high
    God, * and kept not his testimonies;
But turned their backs, and fell away like their
    forefathers; * starting aside like a broken bow.
For they grieved him with their hill-altars, * and
    provoked him to displeasure with their images.
When God heard this, he was wroth, * and took
    sore displeasure at Israel.
So that he forsook the tabernacle in Silo, * even
    the tent that he had pitched among men.
He delivered their power into captivity, * and their
    beauty into the enemy's hand.
He gave his people over also unto the sword, *
    and was wroth with his inheritance.
The fire consumed their young men, * and their
    maidens were not given to marriage.

Their priests were slain with the sword, * and
there were no widows to make lamentation.

So the Lord awaked as one out of sleep, * and like
a giant refreshed with wine.

He smote his enemies in the hinder parts, * and
put them to a perpetual shame.

He refused the tabernacle of Joseph, * and chose
not the tribe of Ephraim;

But chose the tribe of Judah, * even the hill of
Sion which he loved.

And there he built his temple on high, * and laid
the foundation of it like the ground which he
hath made continually.

He chose David also his servant, * and took him
away from the sheep-folds.

As he was following the ewes great with young
ones he took him, * that he might feed Jacob his
people, and Israel his inheritance.

So he fed them with a faithful and true heart, *
and ruled them prudently with all his power.

Psalm 79. *Deus, venerunt.*

A psalm for Asaph.

O GOD, the heathen are come into thine
   inheritance; * thy holy temple have they
   defiled, and made Jerusalem an heap of stones.

The dead bodies of thy servants have they given to
   be meat unto the fowls of the air, * and the
   flesh of thy saints unto the beasts of the land.

Their blood have they shed like water on every
   side of Jerusalem, * and there was no man to
   bury them.

We are become an open shame to our enemies, * a
   very scorn and derision unto them that are
   round about us.

Lord, how long wilt thou be angry? * shall thy
   jealousy burn like fire for ever?

Pour out thine indignation upon the heathen that
   have not known thee; * and upon the kingdoms
   that have not called upon thy Name.

For they have devoured Jacob, * and laid waste
   his dwelling-place.

O remember not our old sins, but have mercy upon us, and that soon; * for we are come to great misery.

Help us, O God of our salvation, for the glory of thy Name: * O deliver us, and be merciful unto our sins, for thy Name's sake.

Wherefore do the heathen say, * Where is now their God?

O let the vengeance of thy servants' blood that is shed, * be openly shewed upon the heathen in our sight.

O let the sorrowful sighing of the prisoners come before thee; * according to the greatness of thy power, preserve thou those that are appointed to die.

And for the blasphemy wherewith our neighbours have blasphemed thee, * reward thou them, O Lord, seven-fold into their bosom.

So we, that are thy people, and sheep of thy pasture, shall give thee thanks for ever, * and will alway be shewing forth thy praise from generation to generation.

Psalm 80. *Qui regis Israël.*

For the end. For alternate verses. A testimony for Asaph:

a Psalm concerning the Assyrian.

HEAR, O thou Shepherd of Israel, thou that leadest Joseph like a sheep; * shew thyself also, thou that sittest upon the cherubims.

Before Ephraim, Benjamin, and Manasses, * stir up thy strength, and come, and help us.

Turn us again, O God; * shew the light of thy countenance, and we shall be whole.

O Lord God of hosts, * how long wilt thou be angry with thy people that prayeth?

Thou feedest them with the bread of tears, * and givest them plenteousness of tears to drink.

Thou hast made us a very strife unto our neighbours, * and our enemies laugh us to scorn.

Turn us again, thou God of hosts; * shew the light of thy countenance, and we shall be whole.

Thou hast brought a vine out of Egypt; * thou hast cast out the heathen, and planted it.

Thou madest room for it; * and when it had taken root it filled the land.

The hills were covered with the shadow of it, *
and the boughs thereof were like the goodly
cedar-trees.

She stretched out her branches unto the sea, * and
her boughs unto the river.

Why hast thou then broken down her hedge, * that
all they that go by pluck off her grapes?

The wild boar out of the wood doth root it up, *
and the wild beasts of the field devour it.

Turn thee again, thou God of hosts, look down
from heaven, * behold, and visit this vine;

And the place of the vineyard that thy right hand
hath planted, * and the branch that thou madest
so strong for thyself.

It is burnt with fire, and cut down; * and they shall
perish at the rebuke of thy countenance.

Let thy hand be upon the man of thy right hand, *
and upon the son of man, whom thou madest so
strong for thine own self.

And so will not we go back from thee: * O let us
live, and we shall call upon thy Name.

Turn us again, O Lord God of hosts; * shew the
light of thy countenance, and we shall be
whole.

Psalm 81. *Exultate Deo.*

For the end. A psalm for Asaph, concerning the winepresses.

SING we merrily unto God our strength; * make a cheerful noise unto the God of Jacob.

Take the psalm, bring hither the tabret, * the merry harp with the lute.

Blow up the trumpet in the new-moon, * even in the time appointed, and upon our solemn feast-day.

For this was made a statute for Israel, * and a law of the God of Jacob.

This he ordained in Joseph for a testimony, * when he came out of the land of Egypt, and had heard a strange language.

I eased his shoulder from the burden, * and his hands were delivered from making the pots.

Thou calledst upon me in troubles, and I delivered thee; * and heard thee what time as the storm fell upon thee.

I proved thee also * at the waters of strife.

Hear, O my people, and I will assure thee, O Israel, * if thou wilt hearken unto me,

There shall no strange god be in thee, * neither
shalt thou worship any other god.

I am the Lord thy God, who brought thee out of
the land of Egypt: * open thy mouth wide, and I
shall fill it.

But my people would not hear my voice; * and
Israel would not obey me.

So I gave them up unto their own hearts' lusts, *
and let them follow their own imaginations.

O that my people would have hearkened unto
me! * for if Israel had walked in my ways,

I should soon have put down their enemies, * and
turned my hand against their adversaries.

The haters of the Lord should have been found
liars; * but their time should have endured for
ever.

He should have fed them also with the finest
wheat-flour; * and with honey out of the stony
rock should I have satisfied thee.

✠ THIRD STASIS ✠

Psalm 82. *Deus stetit.*

A psalm for Asaph.

GOD standeth in the congregation of princes; * he is a Judge among gods.

How long will ye give wrong judgement, * and accept the persons of the ungodly?

Defend the poor and fatherless; * see that such as are in need and necessity have right.

Deliver the outcast and poor; * save them from the hand of the ungodly.

They will not be learned nor understand, but walk on still in darkness: * all the foundations of the earth are out of course.

I have said, Ye are gods, * and ye are all the children of the most Highest.

But ye shall die like men, * and fall like one of the princes.

Arise, O God, and judge thou the earth; * for thou shalt take all heathen to thine inheritance.

Psalm 83. *Deus, quis similis?*

A song of a psalm for Asaph.

HOLD not thy tongue, O God, keep not still
    silence: * refrain not thyself, O God.

For lo, thine enemies make a murmuring; * and
    they that hate thee have lift up their head.

They have imagined craftily against thy people, *
    and taken counsel against thy secret ones.

They have said, Come, and let us root them out,
    that they be no more a people, * and that the
    name of Israel may be no more in
    remembrance.

For they have cast their heads together with one
    consent, * and are confederate against thee;

The tabernacles of the Edomites, and the
    Ismaelites; * the Moabites and Hagarenes;

Gebal, and Ammon, and Amalek; * the
    Philistines, with them that dwell at Tyre.

Assur also is joined with them; * and have holpen
    the children of Lot.

But do thou to them as unto the Madianites; *
    unto Sisera, and unto Jabin at the brook of
    Kison;

Who perished at Endor, * and became as the dung
of the earth.

Make them and their princes like Oreb and Zeb; *
yea, make all their princes like as Zeba and
Salmana;

Who say, Let us take to ourselves * the houses of
God in possession.

O my God, make them like unto a wheel, * and as
the stubble before the wind;

Like as the fire that burneth up the wood, * and as
the flame that consumeth the mountains.

Persecute them even so with thy tempest, * and
make them afraid with thy storm.

Make their faces ashamed, O Lord, * that they
may seek thy Name.

Let them be confounded and vexed ever more and
more; * let them be put to shame, and perish.

And they shall know that thou, whose Name is
Jehovah, * art only the most Highest over all
the earth.

Psalm 84. *Quam dilecta!*

For the end. A song for the sons of Core, concerning the winepresses.

O HOW amiable are thy dwellings, * thou Lord of hosts!

My soul hath a desire and longing to enter into the courts of the Lord; * my heart and my flesh rejoice in the living God.

Yea, the sparrow hath found her an house, and the swallow a nest where she may lay her young; * even thy altars, O Lord of hosts, my King and my God.

Blessed are they that dwell in thy house; * they will be alway praising thee.

Blessed is the man whose strength is in thee; * in whose heart are thy ways.

Who going through the vale of misery use it for a well; * and the pools are filled with water.

They will go from strength to strength, * and unto the God of gods appeareth every one of them in Sion.

O Lord God of hosts, hear my prayer; * hearken, O God of Jacob.

Behold, O God our defender, * and look upon the face of thine Anointed.

For one day in thy courts * is better than a thousand.

I had rather be a door-keeper in the house of my God, * than to dwell in the tents of ungodliness.

For the Lord God is a light and defence; * the Lord will give grace and worship, and no good thing shall he withhold from them that live a godly life.

O Lord God of hosts, * blessed is the man that putteth his trust in thee.

Psalm 85. *Benedixisti, Domine.*

For the end. A psalm for the sons of Core.

LORD, thou art become gracious unto thy land; * thou hast turned away the captivity of Jacob.

Thou hast forgiven the offence of thy people, * and covered all their sins.

Thou hast taken away all thy displeasure, * and turned thyself from thy wrathful indignation.

Turn us then, O God our Saviour, * and let thine anger cease from us.

Wilt thou be displeased at us for ever? * and wilt thou stretch out thy wrath from one generation to another?

Wilt thou not turn again, and quicken us, * that thy people may rejoice in thee?

Shew us thy mercy, O Lord, * and grant us thy salvation.

I will hearken what the Lord God will say concerning me; * for he shall speak peace unto his people, and to his saints, that they turn not again.

For his salvation is nigh them that fear him; * that glory may dwell in our land.

Mercy and truth are met together: * righteousness and peace have kissed each other.

Truth shall flourish out of the earth, * and righteousness hath looked down from heaven.

Yea, the Lord shall shew loving-kindness; * and our land shall give her increase.

Righteousness shall go before him, * and he shall direct his going in the way.

THE TWELFTH KATHISMA

✠ FIRST STASIS ✠

Psalm 86. *Inclina, Domine.*

A prayer of David.

Bow down thine ear, O Lord, and hear me; * for I
am poor, and in misery.

Preserve thou my soul, for I am holy: * my God,
save thy servant that putteth his trust in thee.

Be merciful unto me, O Lord; * for I will call
daily upon thee.

Comfort the soul of thy servant; * for unto thee, O
Lord, do I lift up my soul.

For thou, Lord, art good and gracious, * and of
great mercy unto all them that call upon thee.

Give ear, Lord, unto my prayer, * and ponder the
voice of my humble desires.

In the time of my trouble I will call upon thee; *
for thou hearest me.

Among the gods there is none like unto thee, O
Lord; * there is not one that can do as thou
doest.

All nations whom thou hadst made shall come and
worship thee, O Lord; * and shall glorify thy
Name.
For thou art great, and doest wondrous things: *
thou art God alone.
Teach me thy way, O Lord, and I will walk in thy
truth: * O knit my heart unto thee, that I may
fear thy Name.
I will thank thee, O Lord my God, with all my
heart; * and will praise thy Name for evermore.
For great is thy mercy toward me; * and thou hast
delivered my soul from the nethermost hell.
O God, the proud are risen against me; * and the
congregations of naughty men have sought after
my soul, and have not set thee before their eyes.
But thou, O Lord God, art full of compassion and
mercy, * long-suffering, plenteous in goodness
and truth.
O turn thee then unto me, and have mercy upon
me; * give thy strength unto thy servant, and
help the son of thine handmaid.
Shew some token upon me for good, that they
who hate me may see it and be ashamed, *

because thou, Lord, hast holpen me and comforted me.

Psalm 87. *Fundamenta ejus.*
A psalm of a song for the sons of Core.

HER foundations are upon the holy hills: * the Lord loveth the gates of Sion more than all the dwellings of Jacob.

Very excellent things are spoken of thee, * thou city of God.

I will think upon Rahab and Babylon, * with them that know me.

Behold ye the Philistines also, * and they of Tyre, with the Morians; lo, there was he born.

And of Sion it shall be reported that he was born in her; * and the most High shall stablish her.

The Lord shall rehearse it when he writeth up the people; * that he was born there.

The singers also and trumpeters shall he rehearse: * All my fresh springs shall be in thee.

Psalm 88. *Domine Deus.*

*A song of a psalm for the sons of Core. For the
end. Upon Maheleth, for responsive strains.
Concerning instruction for Æman the Israelite.*

O LORD God of my salvation, I have cried day
and night before thee: * O let my prayer enter
into thy presence, incline thine ear unto my
calling.

For my soul is full of trouble, * and my life
draweth nigh unto hell.

I am counted as one of them that go down into the
pit, * and I have been even as a man that hath
no strength.

Free among the dead, like unto them that are
wounded, and lie in the grave, * who are out of
remembrance, and are cut away from thy hand.

Thou hast laid me in the lowest pit, * in a place of
darkness, and in the deep.

Thine indignation lieth hard upon me, * and thou
hast vexed me with all thy storms.

Thou hast put away mine acquaintance far from
me, * and made me to be abhorred of them.

I am so fast in prison * that I cannot get forth.

My sight faileth for very trouble; * Lord, I have
called daily upon thee, I have stretched forth
my hands unto thee.

Dost thou shew wonders among the dead? * or
shall the dead rise up again, and praise thee?

Shall thy loving-kindness be shewed in the
grave? * or thy faithfulness in destruction?

Shall thy wondrous works be known in the
dark? * and thy righteousness in the land where
all things are forgotten?

Unto thee have I cried, O Lord; * and early shall
my prayer come before thee.

Lord, why abhorrest thou my soul, * and hidest
thou thy face from me?

I am in misery, and like unto him that is at the
point to die; * even from my youth up thy
terrors have I suffered with a troubled mind.

Thy wrathful displeasure goeth over me, * and the
fear of thee hath undone me.

They came round about me daily like water, * and
compassed me together on every side.

My lovers and friends hast thou put away from
me, * and hid mine acquaintance out of my
sight.

Psalm 89. *Misericordias Domini.*

A psalm of instruction for Ætham the Israelite.

MY SONG shall be alway of the loving-kindness of the Lord; * with my mouth will I ever be shewing thy truth from one generation to another.

For I have said, Mercy shall be set up for ever; * thy truth shalt thou stablish in the heavens.

I have made a covenant with my chosen; * I have sworn unto David my servant;

Thy seed will I stablish for ever, * and set up thy throne from one generation to another.

O Lord, the very heavens shall praise thy wondrous works; * and thy truth in the congregation of the saints.

For who is he among the clouds, * that shall be compared unto the Lord?

And what is he among the gods, * that shall be like unto the Lord?

God is very greatly to be feared in the council of the saints, * and to be had in reverence of all them that are round about him.

O Lord God of hosts, who is like unto thee? * thy
truth, most mighty Lord, is on every side.

Thou rulest the raging of the sea; * thou stillest
the waves thereof when they arise.

Thou hast subdued Egypt, and destroyed it; * thou
hast scattered thine enemies abroad with thy
mighty arm.

The heavens are thine, the earth also is thine; *
thou hast laid the foundation of the round
world, and all that therein is.

Thou hast made the north and the south; * Tabor
and Hermon shall rejoice in thy Name.

Thou hast a mighty arm; * strong is thy hand, and
high is thy right hand.

Righteousness and equity are the habitation of thy
seat; * mercy and truth shall go before thy face.

Blessed is the people, O Lord, that can rejoice in
thee; * they shall walk in the light of thy
countenance.

Their delight shall be daily in thy Name; * and in
thy righteousness shall they make their boast.

For thou art the glory of their strength, * and in
thy loving-kindness thou shalt lift up our horns.

For the Lord is our defence; * the Holy One of
Israel is our King.

Thou spakest sometime in visions unto thy saints,
and saidst, * I have laid help upon one that is
mighty; I have exalted one chosen out of the
people.

I have found David my servant; * with my holy
oil have I anointed him.

My hand shall hold him fast, * and my arm shall
strengthen him.

The enemy shall not be able to do him violence; *
the son of wickedness shall not hurt him.

I will smite down his foes before his face, * and
plague them that hate him.

My truth also and my mercy shall be with him; *
and in my Name shall his horn be exalted.

I will set his dominion also in the sea, * and his
right hand in the floods.

He shall call me, Thou art my Father, * my God,
and my strong salvation.

And I will make him my first-born, * higher than
the kings of the earth.

My mercy will I keep for him for evermore, * and
my covenant shall stand fast with him.

His seed also will I make to endure for ever, * and
his throne as the days of heaven.

But if his children forsake my law, * and walk not
in my judgements;

If they break my statutes, and keep not my
commandments; * I will visit their offences
with the rod, and their sin with scourges.

Nevertheless, my loving-kindness will I not
utterly take from him, * nor suffer my truth to
fail.

My covenant I will not break, nor alter the thing
that is gone out of my lips: * I have sworn once
by my holiness, that I will not fail David.

His seed shall endure for ever, * and his seat is
like as the sun before me.

He shall stand fast for evermore as the moon, *
and as the faithful witness in heaven.

But thou hast abhorred and forsaken thine
Anointed, * and art displeased at him.

Thou hast broken the covenant of thy servant, *
and cast his crown to the ground.

Thou hast overthrown all his hedges, * and broken
down his strong holds.

All they that go by spoil him, * and he is become
a reproach to his neighbours.

Thou hast set up the right hand of his enemies, *
and made all his adversaries to rejoice.

Thou hast taken away the edge of his sword, * and
givest him not victory in the battle.

Thou hast put out his glory, * and cast his throne
down to the ground.

The days of his youth hast thou shortened, * and
covered him with dishonour.

Lord, how long wilt thou hide thyself, for ever? *
and shall thy wrath burn like fire?

O remember how short my time is; * wherefore
hast thou made all men for nought?

What man is he that liveth, and shall not see
death? * and shall he deliver his soul from the
hand of hell?

Lord, where are thy old loving-kindnesses, *
which thou swarest unto David in thy truth?

Remember, Lord, the rebuke that thy servants
have, * and how I do bear in my bosom the
rebukes of many people.

Wherewith thine enemies have blasphemed thee,
and slandered the footsteps of thine Anointed. *

Praised be the Lord for evermore. Amen, and Amen.

✠ THIRD STASIS ✠

Psalm 90. *Domine, refugium.*
A prayer of Moses the man of God.

LORD, thou hast been our refuge, * from one generation to another.

Before the mountains were brought forth, or ever the earth and the world were made, * thou art God from everlasting, and world without end.

Thou turnest man to destruction; * again thou sayest, Come again, ye children of men.

For a thousand years in thy sight are but as yesterday; * seeing that is past as a watch in the night.

As soon as thou scatterest them they are even as a sleep; * and fade away suddenly like the grass.

In the morning it is green, and groweth up; * but in the evening it is cut down, dried up, and withered.

For we consume away in thy displeasure, * and are afraid at thy wrathful indignation.

Thou hast set our misdeeds before thee; * and our secret sins in the light of thy countenance.

For when thou art angry all our days are gone: * we bring our years to an end, as it were a tale that is told.

The days of our age are threescore years and ten; and though men be so strong that they come to fourscore years, * yet is their strength then but labour and sorrow; so soon passeth it away, and we are gone.

But who regardeth the power of thy wrath? * for even thereafter as a man feareth, so is thy displeasure.

So teach us to number our days, * that we may apply our hearts unto wisdom.

Turn thee again, O Lord, at the last, * and be gracious unto thy servants.

O satisfy us with thy mercy, and that soon: * so shall we rejoice and be glad all the days of our life.

Comfort us again now after the time that thou hast plagued us; * and for the years wherein we have suffered adversity.

Shew thy servants thy work, * and their children thy glory.

And the glorious majesty of the Lord our God be upon us: * prosper thou the work of our hands upon us, O prosper thou our handywork.

Psalm 91. *Qui habitat.*

The praise of a song, by David.

WHOSO dwelleth under the defence of the most High, * shall abide under the shadow of the Almighty.

I will say unto the Lord, Thou art my hope, and my strong hold; * my God, in him will I trust.

For he shall deliver thee from the snare of the hunter, * and from the noisome pestilence.

He shall defend thee under his wings, and thou shalt be safe under his feathers; * his faithfulness and truth shall be thy shield and buckler.

Thou shalt not be afraid for any terror by night, * nor for the arrow that flieth by day;

For the pestilence that walketh in darkness, * nor for the sickness that destroyeth in the noon-day.

A thousand shall fall beside thee, and ten thousand at thy right hand; * but it shall not come nigh thee.

Yea, with thine eyes shalt thou behold, * and see the reward of the ungodly.

For thou, Lord, art my hope; * thou hast set thine house of defence very high.

There shall no evil happen unto thee, * neither shall any plague come nigh thy dwelling.

For he shall give his angels charge over thee, * to keep thee in all thy ways.

They shall bear thee in their hands, * that thou hurt not thy foot against a stone.

Thou shalt go upon the lion and adder: * the young lion and the dragon shalt thou tread under thy feet.

Because he hath set his love upon me, therefore will I deliver him; * I will set him up, because he hath known my Name.

He shall call upon me, and I will hear him; * yea, I am with him in trouble; I will deliver him, and bring him to honour.

With long life will I satisfy him, * and shew him my salvation.

THE THIRTEENTH KATHISMA

✠ FIRST STASIS ✠

Psalm 92. *Bonum est confiteri.*
A psalm of a song for the Sabbath-day.

IT IS a good thing to give thanks unto the Lord, *
and to sing praises unto thy Name, O most
Highest;

To tell of thy loving-kindness early in the
morning, * and of thy truth in the night-season;

Upon an instrument of ten strings, and upon the
lute; * upon a loud instrument, and upon the
harp.

For thou, Lord, hast made me glad through thy
works; * and I will rejoice in giving praise for
the operations of thy hands.

O Lord, how glorious are thy works! * thy
thoughts are very deep.

An unwise man doth not well consider this, * and
a fool doth not understand it.

When the ungodly are green as the grass, and
  when all the workers of wickedness do
  flourish, * then shall they be destroyed for ever;
  but thou, Lord, art the most Highest for
  evermore.
For lo, thine enemies, O Lord, lo, thine enemies
  shall perish; * and all the workers of
  wickedness shall be destroyed.
But mine horn shall be exalted like the horn of an
  unicorn; * for I am anointed with fresh oil.
Mine eye also shall see his lust of mine enemies, *
  and mine ear shall hear his desire of the wicked
  that arise up against me.
The righteous shall flourish like a palm-tree, * and
  shall spread abroad like a cedar in Libanus.
Such as are planted in the house of the Lord, *
  shall flourish in the courts of the house of our
  God.
They also shall bring forth more fruit in their
  age, * and shall be fat and well-liking.
That they may shew how true the Lord my
  strength is, * and that there is no
  unrighteousness in him.

Psalm 93. *Dominus regnavit.*

For the day before the Sabbath. When the land was first inhabited, the praise of a song by David.

THE Lord is King, and hath put on glorious apparel; * the Lord hath put on his apparel, and girded himself with strength.

He hath made the round world so sure, * that it cannot be moved.

Ever since the world began hath thy seat been prepared: * thou art from everlasting.

The floods are risen, O Lord, the floods have lift up their voice; * the floods lift up their waves.

The waves of the sea are mighty, and rage horribly; * but yet the Lord, who dwelleth on high, is mightier.

Thy testimonies, O Lord, are very sure: * holiness becometh thine house for ever.

Psalm 94. *Deus ultionum.*

A psalm of David for the fourth day of the week.

O LORD God, to whom vengeance belongeth, * thou God, to whom vengeance belongeth, shew thyself.

Arise, thou Judge of the world, * and reward the
 proud after their deserving.
Lord, how long shall the ungodly, * how long
 shall the ungodly triumph?
How long shall all wicked doers speak so
 disdainfully, * and make such proud boasting?
They smite down thy people, O Lord, * and
 trouble thine heritage.
They murder the widow and the stranger, * and
 put the fatherless to death.
And yet they say, Tush, the Lord shall not see, *
 neither shall the God of Jacob regard it.
Take heed, ye unwise among the people: * O ye
 fools, when will ye understand?
He that planted the ear, shall he not hear? * or he
 that made the eye, shall he not see?
Or he that nurtureth the heathen, * it is he that
 teacheth man knowledge, shall not he punish?
The Lord knoweth the thoughts of man, * that
 they are but vain.
Blessed is the man whom thou chastenest,
 O Lord, * and teachest him in thy law;

That thou mayest give him patience in time of
adversity, * until the pit be digged up for the
ungodly.
For the Lord will not fail his people; * neither will
he forsake his inheritance;
Until righteousness turn again unto judgement: *
all such as are true in heart shall follow it.
Who will rise up with me against the wicked? * or
who will take my part against the evil-doers?
If the Lord had not helped me, * it had not failed
but my soul had been put to silence.
But when I said, My foot hath slipt; * thy mercy,
O Lord, held me up.
In the multitude of the sorrows that I had in my
heart, * thy comforts have refreshed my soul.
Wilt thou have any thing to do with the stool of
wickedness, * which imagineth mischief as a
law?
They gather them together against the soul of the
righteous, * and condemn the innocent blood.
But the Lord is my refuge, * and my God is the
strength of my confidence.

He shall recompense them their wickedness, and
destroy them in their own malice; * yea, the
Lord our God shall destroy them.

✠ SECOND STASIS ✠

Psalm 95. *Venite, exultemus.*
The praise of a song, by David.

O COME, let us sing unto the Lord, * let us heartily
rejoice in the strength of our salvation.

Let us come before his presence with
thanksgiving, * and shew ourselves glad in him
with psalms.

For the Lord is a great God, * and a great King
above all gods.

In his hand are all the corners of the earth, * and
the strength of the hills is his also.

The sea is his, and he made it, * and his hands
prepared the dry land.

O come, let us worship and fall down, * and kneel
before the Lord our Maker.

For he is the Lord our God; * and we are the
people of his pasture, and the sheep of his hand.

To-day if ye will hear his voice, harden not your
    hearts, * as in the provocation, and as in the day
    of temptation in the wilderness.
When your fathers tempted me, * proved me, and
    saw my works.
Forty years long was I grieved with this
    generation, and said: * It is a people that do err
    in their hearts, for they have not known my
    ways;
Unto whom I sware in my wrath * that they
    should not enter into my rest.

Psalm 96. *Cantate Domino.*

When the house was built after the captivity. A
song by David.

O SING unto the Lord a new song; * sing unto the
    Lord, all the whole earth.
Sing unto the Lord, and praise his Name; * be
    telling of his salvation from day to day.
Declare his honour unto the heathen, * and his
    wonders unto all people.
For the Lord is great, and cannot worthily be
    praised; * he is more to be feared than all gods.

As for all the gods of the heathen, they are but
idols; * but it is the Lord that made the heavens.

Glory and worship are before him; * power and
honour are in his sanctuary.

Ascribe unto the Lord, O ye kindreds of the
people, * ascribe unto the Lord worship and
power.

Ascribe unto the Lord the honour due unto his
Name; * bring presents, and come into his
courts.

O worship the Lord in the beauty of holiness; * let
the whole earth stand in awe of him.

Tell it out among the heathen that the Lord is
King, * and that it is he who hath made the
round world so fast that it cannot be moved;
and how that he shall judge the people
righteously.

Let the heavens rejoice, and let the earth be
glad; * let the sea make a noise, and all that
therein is.

Let the field be joyful, and all that is in it; * then
shall all the trees of the wood rejoice before the
Lord.

For he cometh, for he cometh to judge the earth; *
and with righteousness to judge the world, and
the people with his truth.

Psalm 97. *Dominus regnavit.*
For David, when his land is established.

THE Lord is King, the earth may be glad
thereof; * yea, the multitude of the isles may be
glad thereof.

Clouds and darkness are round about him: *
righteousness and judgement are the habitation
of his seat.

There shall go a fire before him, * and burn up his
enemies on every side.

His lightnings gave shine unto the world: * the
earth saw it, and was afraid.

The hills melted like wax at the presence of the
Lord; * at the presence of the Lord of the whole
earth.

The heavens have declared his righteousness, *
and all the people have seen his glory.

Confounded be all they that worship carved
images, and that delight in vain gods: * worship
him, all ye gods.

Sion heard of it, and rejoiced; * and the daughters
of Judah were glad, because of thy judgements,
O Lord.
For thou, Lord, art higher than all that are in the
earth: * thou art exalted far above all gods.
O ye that love the Lord, see that ye hate the thing
which is evil: * the Lord preserveth the souls of
his saints; he shall deliver them from the hand
of the ungodly.
There is sprung up a light for the righteous, * and
joyful gladness for such as are true-hearted.
Rejoice in the Lord, ye righteous; * and give
thanks for a remembrance of his holiness.

Psalm 98. *Cantate Domino.*
A psalm of David.

O SING unto the Lord a new song; * for he hath done marvellous things.

With his own right hand, and with his holy arm, * hath he gotten himself the victory.

The Lord declared his salvation; * his righteousness hath he openly shewed in the sight of the heathen.

He hath remembered his mercy and truth toward the house of Israel; * and all the ends of the world have seen the salvation of our God.

Shew yourselves joyful unto the Lord, all ye lands; * sing, rejoice, and give thanks.

Praise the Lord upon the harp; * sing to the harp with a psalm of thanksgiving.

With trumpets also and shawms, * O shew yourselves joyful before the Lord the King.

Let the sea make a noise, and all that therein is; * the round world, and they that dwell therein.

Let the floods clap their hands, and let the hills be
  joyful together before the Lord; * for he is
  come to judge the earth.
With righteousness shall he judge the world, * and
  the people with equity.

Psalm 99. *Dominus regnavit.*
A psalm of David.

THE Lord is King, be the people never so
  unpatient; * he sitteth between the cherubims,
  be the earth never so unquiet.
The Lord is great in Sion, * and high above all
  people.
They shall give thanks unto thy Name, * which is
  great, wonderful, and holy.
The King's power loveth judgement; thou hast
  prepared equity, * thou hast executed
  judgement and righteousness in Jacob.
O magnify the Lord our God; * and fall down
  before his footstool, for he is holy.
Moses and Aaron among his priests, and Samuel
  among such as call upon his Name: * these
  called upon the Lord, and he heard them.

He spake unto them out of the cloudy pillar; * for they kept his testimonies, and the law that he gave them.

Thou heardest them, O Lord our God; * thou forgavest them, O God, and punishedst their own inventions.

O magnify the Lord our God, and worship him upon his holy hill; * for the Lord our God is holy.

Psalm 100. *Jubilate Deo.*
A psalm for thanksgiving.

O BE joyful in the Lord, all ye lands: * serve the Lord with gladness, and come before his presence with a song.

Be ye sure that the Lord he is God; * it is he that hath made us, and not we ourselves; we are his people, and the sheep of his pasture.

O go your way into his gates with thanksgiving, and into his courts with praise; * be thankful unto him, and speak good of his Name.

For the Lord is gracious, his mercy is everlasting; * and his truth endureth from generation to generation.

Psalm 101. *Misericordiam et judicium.*

A psalm of David.

MY SONG shall be of mercy and judgement; * unto
thee, O Lord, will I sing.

O let me have understanding * in the way of
godliness.

When wilt thou come unto me? * I will walk in
my house with a perfect heart.

I will take no wicked thing in hand; I hate the sins
of unfaithfulness; * there shall no such cleave
unto me.

A froward heart shall depart from me; * I will not
know a wicked person.

Whoso privily slandereth his neighbour, * him
will I destroy.

Whoso hath also a proud look and high stomach, *
I will not suffer him.

Mine eyes look upon such as are faithful in the
land, * that they may dwell with me.

Whoso leadeth a godly life, * he shall be my
servant.

There shall no deceitful person dwell in my
house; * he that telleth lies shall not tarry in my
sight.
I shall soon destroy all the ungodly that are in the
land; * that I may root out all wicked doers
from the city of the Lord.

THE FOURTEENTH KATHISMA

✠ FIRST STASIS ✠

Psalm 102. *Domine, exaudi.*

A prayer for the poor, when he is deeply afflicted and poureth out his supplication before the Lord.

HEAR my prayer, O Lord, * and let my crying
come unto thee.

Hide not thy face from me in the time of my
trouble; * incline thine ear unto me when I call;
O hear me, and that right soon.

For my days are consumed away like smoke, *
and my bones are burnt up as it were a
firebrand.

My heart is smitten down, and withered liked
grass; * so that I forget to eat my bread.

For the voice of my groaning, * my bones will
scarce cleave to my flesh.

I am become like a pelican in the wilderness, *
and like an owl that is in the desert.

I have watched, and am even as it were a
sparrow, * that sitteth alone upon the house-top.

Mine enemies revile me all the day long; * and
   they that are mad upon me are sworn together
   against me.
For I have eaten ashes as it were bread, * and
   mingled my drink with weeping;
And that because of thine indignation and wrath; *
   for thou hast taken me up, and cast me down.
My days are gone like a shadow, * and I am
   withered like grass.
But thou, O Lord, shalt endure for ever, * and thy
   remembrance throughout all generations.
Thou shalt arise, and have mercy upon Sion; * for
   it is time that thou have mercy upon her, yea,
   the time is come.
And why? thy servants think upon her stones, *
   and it pitieth them to see her in the dust.
The heathen shall fear thy Name, O Lord; * and
   all the kings of the earth thy majesty;
When the Lord shall build up Sion, * and when
   his glory shall appear;
When he turneth him unto the prayer of the poor
   destitute, * and despiseth not their desire.

This shall be written for those that come after, *
and the people which shall be born shall praise
the Lord.

For he hath looked down from his sanctuary; * out
of the heaven did the Lord behold the earth;

That he might hear the mournings of such as are
in captivity, * and deliver the children
appointed unto death;

That they may declare the Name of the Lord in
Sion, * and his worship at Jerusalem;

When the people are gathered together, * and the
kingdoms also, to serve the Lord.

He brought down my strength in my journey, *
and shortened my days.

But I said, O my God, take me not away in the
midst of mine age; * as for thy years, they
endure throughout all generations.

Thou, Lord, in the beginning hast laid the
foundation of the earth, * and the heavens are
the work of thy hands.

They shall perish, but thou shalt endure: * they all
shall wax old as doth a garment;

And as a vesture shalt thou change them, and they
   shall be changed; * but thou art the same, and
   thy years shall not fail.
The children of thy servants shall continue, * and
   their seed shall stand fast in thy sight.

Psalm 103. *Benedic, anima mea.*
A psalm of David.

PRAISE the Lord, O my soul; * and all that is
   within me praise his holy Name.
Praise the Lord, O my soul, * and forget not all his
   benefits;
Who forgiveth all thy sin, * and healeth all thine
   infirmities;
Who saveth thy life from destruction, * and
   crowneth thee with mercy and loving-kindness;
Who satisfieth thy mouth with good things, *
   making thee young and lusty as an eagle.
The Lord executeth righteousness and judgement
   * for all them that are oppressed with wrong.
He shewed his ways unto Moses, * his works unto
   the children of Israel.
The Lord is full of compassion and mercy, * long-
   suffering, and of great goodness.

He will not alway be chiding; * neither keepeth he
his anger for ever.

He hath not dealt with us after our sins; * nor
rewarded us according to our wickednesses.

For look how high the heaven is in comparison of
the earth; * so great is his mercy also toward
them that fear him.

Look how wide also the east is from the west; * so
far hath he set our sins from us.

Yea, like as a father pitieth his own children; *
even so is the Lord merciful unto them that fear
him.

For he knoweth whereof we are made; * he
remembereth that we are but dust.

The days of man are but as grass; * for he
flourisheth as a flower of the field.

For as soon as the wind goeth over it, it is gone; *
and the place thereof shall know it no more.

But the merciful goodness of the Lord endureth
for ever and ever upon them that fear him; *
and his righteousness upon children's children;

Even upon such as keep his covenant, * and think
upon his commandments to do them.

The Lord hath prepared his seat in heaven, * and
his kingdom ruleth over all.

O praise the Lord, ye angels of his, ye that excel
in strength; * ye that fulfil his commandment,
and hearken unto the voice of his words.

O praise the Lord, all ye his hosts; * ye servants of
his that do his pleasure.

O speak good of the Lord, all ye works of his, in
all places of his dominion: * praise thou the
Lord, O my soul.

✠ SECOND STASIS ✠

Psalm 104. *Benedic, anima mea.*
A psalm of David.

PRAISE the Lord, O my soul: * O Lord my God,
thou art become exceeding glorious; thou art
clothed with majesty and honour.

Thou deckest thyself with light as it were with a
garment, * and spreadest out the heavens like a
curtain.

Who layeth the beams of his chambers in the
waters, * and maketh the clouds his chariot, and
walketh upon the wings of the wind.

He maketh his angels spirits, * and his ministers a
flaming fire.

He laid the foundations of the earth, * that it never
should move at any time.

Thou coveredst it with the deep like as with a
garment; * the waters stand in the hills.

At thy rebuke they flee; * at the voice of thy
thunder they are afraid.

They go up as high as the hills, and down to the
valleys beneath; * even unto the place which
thou hast appointed for them.

Thou hast set them their bounds which they shall
not pass, * neither turn again to cover the earth.

He sendeth the springs into the rivers, * which run
among the hills.

All beasts of the field drink thereof, * and the wild
asses quench their thirst.

Beside them shall the fowls of the air have their
habitation, * and sing among the branches.

He watereth the hills from above; * the earth is
filled with the fruit of thy works.

He bringeth forth grass for the cattle, * and green
herb for the service of men;

That he may bring food out of the earth, and wine
that maketh glad the heart of man; * and oil to
make him a cheerful countenance, and bread to
strengthen man's heart.

The trees of the Lord also are full of sap; * even
the cedars of Libanus which he hath planted;

Wherein the birds make their nests; * and the fir-
trees are a dwelling for the stork.

The high hills are a refuge for the wild goats; *
and so are the stony rocks for the conies.

He appointed the moon for certain seasons, * and
the sun knoweth his going down.

Thou makest darkness that it may be night; *
wherein all the beasts of the forest do move.

The lions roaring after their prey, * do seek their
meat from God.

The sun ariseth, and they get them away
together, * and lay them down in their dens.

Man goeth forth to his work, and to his labour, *
until the evening.

O Lord, how manifold are thy works! * in wisdom
hast thou made them all; the earth is full of thy
riches.

So is the great and wide sea also; * wherein are
things creeping innumerable, both small and
great beasts.

There go the ships, and there is that Leviathan, *
whom thou hast made to take his pastime
therein.

These wait all upon thee, * that thou mayest give
them meat in due season.

When thou givest it them they gather it; * and
when thou openest thy hand they are filled with
good.

When thou hidest thy face they are troubled: *
when thou takest away their breath they die,
and are turned again to their dust.

When thou lettest thy breath go forth they shall be
made; * and thou shalt renew the face of the
earth.

The glorious majesty of the Lord shall endure for
ever; * the Lord shall rejoice in his works.

The earth shall tremble at the look of him; * if he
do but touch the hills, they shall smoke.

I will sing unto the Lord as long as I live; * I will
praise my God while I have my being.

And so shall my words please him: * my joy shall be in the Lord.
As for sinners, they shall be consumed out of the earth, and the ungodly shall come to an end; * praise thou the Lord, O my soul, praise the Lord.

✠ THIRD STASIS ✠

Psalm 105. *Confitemini Domino.*
Alleluia.

O GIVE thanks unto the Lord, and call upon his Name; * tell the people what things he hath done.
O let your songs be of him, and praise him; * and let your talking be of all his wondrous works.
Rejoice in his holy Name; * let the heart of them rejoice that seek the Lord.
Seek the Lord and his strength; * seek his face evermore.
Remember the marvellous works that he hath done; * his wonders, and the judgements of his mouth.

O ye seed of Abraham his servant, * ye children
of Jacob his chosen.

He is the Lord our God; * his judgements are in
all the world.

He hath been alway mindful of his covenant and
promise, * that he made to a thousand
generations;

Even the covenant that he made with Abraham; *
and the oath that he sware unto Isaac;

And appointed the same unto Jacob for a law, *
and to Israel for an everlasting testament;

Saying, Unto thee will I give the land of
Canaan, * the lot of your inheritance;

When there were yet but a few of them, * and they
strangers in the land;

What time as they went from one nation to
another, * from one kingdom to another people;

He suffered no man to do them wrong, * but
reproved even kings for their sakes;

Touch not mine Anointed, * and do my prophets
no harm.

Moreover, he called for a dearth upon the land, *
and destroyed all the provision of bread.

But he had sent a man before them, * even Joseph,
    who was sold to be a bond-servant;
Whose feet they hurt in the stocks; * the iron
    entered into his soul;
Until the time came that his cause was known: *
    the word of the Lord tried him.
The king sent, and delivered him; * the prince of
    the people let him go free.
He made him lord also of his house, * and ruler of
    all his substance;
That he might inform his princes after his will, *
    and teach his senators wisdom.
Israel also came into Egypt, * and Jacob was a
    stranger in the land of Ham.
And he increased his people exceedingly, * and
    made them stronger than their enemies;
Whose heart turned, so that they hated his
    people, * and dealt untruly with his servants.
Then sent he Moses his servant, * and Aaron
    whom he had chosen.
And these shewed his tokens among them, * and
    wonders in the land of Ham.
He sent darkness, and it was dark; * and they were
    not obedient unto his word.

He turned their waters into blood, * and slew their fish.

Their land brought forth frogs; * yea, even in their kings' chambers.

He spake the word, and there came all manner of flies, * and lice in all their quarters.

He gave them hail-stones for rain; * and flames of fire in their land.

He smote their vines also and fig-trees; * and destroyed the trees that were in their coasts.

He spake the word, and the grasshoppers came, and caterpillars innumerable, * and did eat up all the grass in their land, and devoured the fruit of their ground.

He smote all the first-born in their land; * even the chief of all their strength.

He brought them forth also with silver and gold; * there was not one feeble person among their tribes.

Egypt was glad at their departing; * for they were afraid of them.

He spread out a cloud to be a covering, * and fire to give light in the night-season.

At their desire he brought quails; * and he filled them with the bread of heaven.

He opened the rock of stone, and the waters flowed out: * so that rivers ran in the dry places.

For why? he remembered his holy promise; * and Abraham his servant.

And he brought forth his people with joy, * and his chosen with gladness;

And gave them the lands of the heathen; * and they took the labours of the people in possession;

That they might keep his statutes, * and observe his laws.

THE FIFTEENTH KATHISMA

✠ FIRST STASIS ✠

Psalm 106. *Confitemini Domino.*
Alleluia.

O GIVE thanks unto the Lord, for he is gracious, *
and his mercy endureth for ever.

Who can express the noble acts of the Lord, * or
shew forth all his praise?

Blessed are they that alway keep judgement, * and
do righteousness.

Remember me, O Lord, according to the favour
that thou bearest unto thy people; * O visit me
with thy salvation;

That I may see the felicity of thy chosen, * and
rejoice in the gladness of thy people, and give
thanks with thine inheritance.

We have sinned with our fathers; * we have done
amiss, and dealt wickedly.

Our fathers regarded not thy wonders in Egypt,
neither kept they thy great goodness in

remembrance; * but were disobedient at the sea, even at the Red sea.

Nevertheless, he helped them for his Name's sake, * that he might make his power to be known.

He rebuked the Red sea also, and it was dried up; * so he led them through the deep, as through a wilderness.

And he saved them from the adversary's hand, * and delivered them from the hand of the enemy.

As for those that troubled them, the waters overwhelmed them; * there was not one of them left.

Then believed they his words, * and sang praise unto him.

But within a while they forgat his works, * and would not abide his counsel.

But lust came upon them in the wilderness, * and they tempted God in the desert.

And he gave them their desire, * and sent leanness withal into their soul.

They angered Moses also in the tents, * and Aaron the saint of the Lord.

So the earth opened, and swallowed up Dathan, * and covered the congregation of Abiram.

And the fire was kindled in their company; * the
　　flame burnt up the ungodly.
They made a calf in Horeb, * and worshipped the
　　molten image.
Thus they turned their glory * into the similitude
　　of a calf that eateth hay.
And they forgat God their Saviour, * who had
　　done so great things in Egypt;
Wondrous works in the land of Ham; * and fearful
　　things by the Red sea.
So he said, he would have destroyed them, had not
　　Moses his chosen stood before him in the gap, *
　　to turn away his wrathful indignation, lest he
　　should destroy them.
Yea, they thought scorn of that pleasant land, *
　　and gave no credence unto his word;
But murmured in their tents, * and hearkened not
　　unto the voice of the Lord.
Then lift he up his hand against them, * to
　　overthrow them in the wilderness;
To cast out their seed among the nations, * and to
　　scatter them in the lands.
They joined themselves unto Baal-peor, * and ate
　　the offerings of the dead.

Thus they provoked him to anger with their own
  inventions; * and the plague was great among
  them.
Then stood up Phinees and prayed; * and so the
  plague ceased.
And that was counted unto him for righteousness,
  * among all posterities for evermore.
They angered him also at the waters of strife, * so
  that he punished Moses for their sakes;
Because they provoked his spirit, * so that he
  spake unadvisedly with his lips.
Neither destroyed they the heathen, * as the Lord
  commanded them;
But were mingled among the heathen, * and
  learned their works.
Insomuch that they worshipped their idols, which
  turned to their own decay; * yea, they offered
  their sons and their daughters unto devils;
And shed innocent blood, even the blood of their
  sons and of their daughters, * whom they had
  offered unto the idols of Canaan; and the land
  was defiled with blood.
Thus were they stained with their own works, *
  and went a whoring with their own inventions.

Therefore was the wrath of the Lord kindled against his people, * insomuch that he abhorred his own inheritance.

And he gave them over into the hands of the heathen; * and they that hated them were lords over them.

Their enemies oppressed them, * and had them in subjection.

Many a time did he deliver them; * but they rebelled against him with their own inventions, and were brought down in their wickedness.

Nevertheless, when he saw their adversity, * he heard their complaint.

He thought upon his covenant, and pitied them according unto the multitude of his mercies; * yea, he made all those that led them away captive to pity them.

Deliver us, O Lord our God, and gather us from among the heathen; * that we may give thanks unto thy holy Name, and make our boast of thy praise.

Blessed be the Lord God of Israel from everlasting and world without end; * and let all the people say, Amen.

Psalm 107. *Confitemini Domino.*
Alleluia.

O GIVE thanks unto the Lord, for he is gracious, *
and his mercy endureth for ever.

Let them give thanks whom the Lord hath
redeemed, * and delivered from the hand of the
enemy;

And gathered them out of the lands, from the east
and from the west; * from the north and from
the south.

They went astray in the wilderness out of the
way, * and found no city to dwell in;

Hungry and thirsty, * their soul fainted in them.

So they cried unto the Lord in their trouble, * and
he delivered them from their distress.

He led them forth by the right way, * that they
might go to the city where they dwelt.

O that men would therefore praise the Lord for his
goodness; * and declare the wonders that he
doeth for the children of men!

For he satisfieth the empty soul, * and filleth the
hungry soul with goodness.

Such as sit in darkness, and in the shadow of
death, * being fast bound in misery and iron;
Because they rebelled against the words of the
Lord, * and lightly regarded the counsel of the
most Highest;
He also brought down their heart through
heaviness: * they fell down, and there was none
to help them.
So when they cried unto the Lord in their
trouble, * he delivered them out of their
distress.
For he brought them out of darkness, and out of
the shadow of death, * and brake their bonds in
sunder.
O that men would therefore praise the Lord for his
goodness; * and declare the wonders that he
doeth for the children of men!
For he hath broken the gates of brass, * and
smitten the bars of iron in sunder.
Foolish men are plagued for their offence, * and
because of their wickedness.
Their soul abhorred all manner of meat, * and
they were even hard at death's door.

So when they cried unto the Lord in their
   trouble, * he delivered them out of their
   distress.
He sent his word, and healed them; * and they
   were saved from their destruction.
O that men would therefore praise the Lord for his
   goodness; * and declare the wonders that he
   doeth for the children of men!
That they would offer unto him the sacrifice of
   thanksgiving, * and tell out his works with
   gladness!
They that go down to the sea in ships, * and
   occupy their business in great waters;
These men see the works of the Lord, * and his
   wonders in the deep.
For at his word the stormy wind ariseth, * which
   lifteth up the waves thereof.
They are carried up to the heaven, and down again
   to the deep; * their soul melteth away because
   of the trouble.
They reel to and fro, and stagger like a drunken
   man, * and are at their wits' end.
So when they cry unto the Lord in their trouble, *
   he delivereth them out of their distress.

For he maketh the storm to cease, * so that the
  waves thereof are still.
Then are they glad, because they are at rest; * and
  so he bringeth them unto the haven where they
  would be.
O that men would therefore praise the Lord for his
  goodness; * and declare the wonders that he
  doeth for the children of men!
That they would exalt him also in the
  congregation of the people, * and praise him in
  the seat of the elders!
Who turneth the floods into a wilderness, * and
  drieth up the water-springs.
A fruitful land maketh he barren, * for the
  wickedness of them that dwell therein.
Again, he maketh the wilderness a standing
  water, * and water-springs of a dry ground.
And there he setteth the hungry, * that they may
  build them a city to dwell in;
That they may sow their land, and plant
  vineyards, * to yield them fruits of increase.
He blesseth them so that they multiply
  exceedingly; * and suffereth not their cattle to
  decrease.

And again, when they are minished and brought
low * through oppression, through any plague
or trouble;

Though he suffer them to be evil intreated through
tyrants, * and let them wander out of the way in
the wilderness;

Yet helpeth he the poor out of misery, * and
maketh him households like a flock of sheep.

The righteous will consider this, and rejoice; * and
the mouth of all wickedness shall be stopped.

Whoso is wise will ponder these things; * and
they shall understand the loving-kindness of the
Lord.

Psalm 108. *Paratum cor meum.*
A song of a psalm by David.

O GOD, my heart is ready, my heart is ready; * I will sing and give praise with the best member that I have.

Awake, thou lute, and harp; * I myself will awake right early.

I will give thanks unto thee, O Lord, among the people; * I will sing praises unto thee among the nations.

For thy mercy is greater than the heavens, * and thy truth reacheth unto the clouds.

Set up thyself, O God, above the heavens, * and thy glory above all the earth.

That thy beloved may be delivered: * let thy right hand save them, and hear thou me.

God hath spoken in his holiness; * I will rejoice therefore, and divide Sichem, and mete out the valley of Succoth.

Gilead is mine, and Manasses is mine; * Ephraim also is the strength of my head.

Judah is my law-giver, Moab is my wash-pot; *
over Edom will I cast out my shoe, upon
Philistia will I triumph.

Who will lead me into the strong city? * and who
will bring me into Edom?

Hast not thou forsaken us, O God? * and wilt not
thou, O God, go forth with our hosts?

O help us against the enemy: * for vain is the help
of man.

Through God we shall do great acts; * and it is he
that shall tread down our enemies.

Psalm 109. *Deus, laudem.*
For the end. A psalm of David.

HOLD not thy tongue, O God of my praise; * for
the mouth of the ungodly, yea, the mouth of the
deceitful is opened upon me.

And they have spoken against me with false
tongues; * they compassed me about also with
words of hatred, and fought against me without
a cause.

For the love that I had unto them, lo, they take
now my contrary part; * but I give myself unto
prayer.

Thus have they rewarded me evil for good, * and hatred for my good will.

Set thou an ungodly man to be ruler over him, * and let Satan stand at his right hand.

When sentence is given upon him, let him be condemned; * and let his prayer be turned into sin.

Let his days be few; * and let another take his office.

Let his children be fatherless, * and his wife a widow.

Let his children be vagabonds, and beg their bread; * let them seek it also out of desolate places.

Let the extortioner consume all that he hath; * and let the stranger spoil his labour.

Let there be no man to pity him, * nor to have compassion upon his fatherless children.

Let his posterity be destroyed; * and in the next generation let his name be clean put out.

Let the wickedness of his fathers be had in remembrance in the sight of the Lord; * and let not the sin of his mother be done away.

Let them alway be before the Lord, * that he may
   root out the memorial of them from off the
   earth.
And that, because his mind was not to do good; *
   but persecuted the poor helpless man, that he
   might slay him that was vexed at the heart.
His delight was in cursing, and it shall happen
   unto him; * he loved not blessing, therefore
   shall it be far from him.
He clothed himself with cursing, like as with a
   raiment, * and it shall come into his bowels like
   water, and like oil into his bones.
Let it be unto him as the cloke that he hath upon
   him, * and as the girdle that he is alway girded
   withal.
Let it thus happen from the Lord unto mine
   enemies, * and to those that speak evil against
   my soul.
But deal thou with me, O Lord God, according
   unto thy Name; * for sweet is thy mercy.
O deliver me, for I am helpless and poor, * and
   my heart is wounded within me.
I go hence like the shadow that departeth, * and
   am driven away as the grasshopper.

My knees are weak through fasting; * my flesh is
dried up for want of fatness.

I became also a reproach unto them: * they that
looked upon me shaked their heads.

Help me, O Lord my God; * O save me according
to thy mercy.

And they shall know, how that this is thy hand, *
and that thou, Lord, hast done it.

Though they curse, yet bless thou; * and let them
be confounded that rise up against me; but let
thy servant rejoice.

Let mine adversaries be clothed with shame; * and
let them cover themselves with their own
confusion, as with a cloke.

As for me, I will give great thanks unto the Lord
with my mouth, * and praise him among the
multitude.

For he shall stand at the right hand of the poor, *
to save his soul from the unrighteous judges.

THE SIXTEENTH KATHISMA

✠ FIRST STASIS ✠

Psalm 110. *Dixit Dominus.*
A psalm of David.

THE Lord said unto my Lord, * Sit thou on my
   right hand, until I make thine enemies thy
   footstool.

The Lord shall send the rod of thy power out of
   Sion: * be thou ruler, even in the midst among
   thine enemies.

In the day of thy power shall the people offer thee
   free-will offerings with an holy worship: * the
   dew of thy birth is of the womb of the morning.

The Lord sware, and will not repent, * Thou art a
   priest for ever after the order of Melchisedech.

The Lord upon thy right hand * shall wound even
   kings in the day of his wrath.

He shall judge among the heathen; * he shall fill
   the places with the dead bodies, and smite in
   sunder the heads over divers countries.

He shall drink of the brook in the way; * therefore shall he lift up his head.

Psalm 111. *Confitebor tibi.*
Alleluia.

I WILL give thanks unto the Lord with my whole heart, * secretly among the faithful, and in the congregation.

The works of the Lord are great, * sought out of all them that have pleasure therein.

His work is worthy to be praised and had in honour, * and his righteousness endureth for ever.

The merciful and gracious Lord hath so done his marvellous works, * that they ought to be had in remembrance.

He hath given meat unto them that fear him; * he shall ever be mindful of his covenant.

He hath shewed his people the power of his works, * that he may give them the heritage of the heathen.

The works of his hands are verity and judgement; * all his commandments are true.

They stand fast for ever and ever, * and are done in truth and equity.

He sent redemption unto his people; * he hath commanded his covenant for ever; holy and reverend is his Name.

The fear of the Lord is the beginning of wisdom; * a good understanding have all they that do thereafter; the praise of it endureth for ever.

Psalm 112. *Beatus vir.*

Alleluia.

BLESSED is the man that feareth the Lord; * he hath great delight in his commandments.

His seed shall be mighty upon earth; * the generation of the faithful shall be blessed.

Riches and plenteousness shall be in his house; * and his righteousness endureth for ever.

Unto the godly there ariseth up light in the darkness; * he is merciful, loving, and righteous.

A good man is merciful, and lendeth; * and will guide his words with discretion.

For he shall never be moved: * and the righteous shall be had in everlasting remembrance.

He will not be afraid of any evil tidings; * for his
  heart standeth fast, and believeth in the Lord.
His heart is established, and will not shrink, *
  until he see his desire upon his enemies.
He hath dispersed abroad, and given to the poor, *
  and his righteousness remaineth for ever; his
  horn shall be exalted with honour.
The ungodly shall see it, and it shall grieve him; *
  he shall gnash with his teeth, and consume
  away; the desire of the ungodly shall perish.

✠ SECOND STASIS ✠

Psalm 113. *Laudate, pueri.*
Alleluia.

PRAISE the Lord, ye servants; * O praise the Name
  of the Lord.
Blessed be the Name of the Lord * from this time
  forth for evermore.
The Lord's Name is praised * from the rising up
  of the sun unto the going down of the same.
The Lord is high above all heathen, * and his
  glory above the heavens.

Who is like unto the Lord our God, that hath his
    dwelling so high, * and yet humbleth himself to
    behold the things that are in heaven and earth?
He taketh up the simple out of the dust, * and
    lifteth the poor out of the mire;
That he may set him with the princes, * even with
    the princes of his people.
He maketh the barren woman to keep house, * and
    to be a joyful mother of children.

Psalm 114. *In exitu Israël.*
Alleluia.

WHEN Israel came out of Egypt, * and the house
    of Jacob from among the strange people,
Judah was his sanctuary, * and Israel his
    dominion.
The sea saw that, and fled; * Jordan was driven
    back.
The mountains skipped like rams, * and the little
    hills like young sheep.
What aileth thee, O thou sea, that thou fleddest? *
    and thou Jordan, that thou wast driven back?
Ye mountains, that ye skipped like rams? * and ye
    little hills, like young sheep?

Tremble, thou earth, at the presence of the Lord; *
at the presence of the God of Jacob;
Who turned the hard rock into a standing water, *
and the flint-stone into a springing well.

Psalm 115. *Non nobis, Domine.*

NOT unto us, O Lord, not unto us, but unto thy
Name give the praise; * for thy loving mercy
and for thy truth's sake.
Wherefore shall the heathen say, * Where is now
their God?
As for our God, he is in heaven: * he hath done
whatsoever pleased him.
Their idols are silver and gold, * even the work of
men's hands.
They have mouths, and speak not; * eyes have
they, and see not.
They have ears, and hear not; * noses have they,
and smell not.
They have hands, and handle not; feet have they,
and walk not; * neither speak they through their
throat.
They that make them are like unto them; * and so
are all such as put their trust in them.

But thou, house of Israel, trust thou in the Lord; *
    he is their succour and defence.
Ye house of Aaron, put your trust in the Lord; *
    he is their helper and defender.
Ye that fear the Lord, put your trust in the Lord; *
    he is their helper and defender.
The Lord hath been mindful of us, and he shall
    bless us; * even he shall bless the house of
    Israel, he shall bless the house of Aaron.
He shall bless them that fear the Lord, * both
    small and great.
The Lord shall increase you more and more, * you
    and your children.
Ye are the blessed of the Lord, * who made
    heaven and earth.
All the whole heavens are the Lord's; * the earth
    hath he given to the children of men.
The dead praise not thee, O Lord, * neither all
    they that go down into silence.
But we will praise the Lord, * from this time forth
    for evermore. Praise the Lord.

✠ THIRD STASIS ✠

Psalm 116. *Dilexi, quoniam.*
Alleluia.

I AM well pleased * that the Lord hath heard the
    voice of my prayer;

That he hath inclined his ear unto me; * therefore
    will I call upon him as long as I live.

The snares of death compassed me round about, *
    and the pains of hell gat hold upon me.

I shall find trouble and heaviness, and I will call
    upon the Name of the Lord; * O Lord, I beseech
    thee, deliver my soul.

Gracious is the Lord, and righteous; * yea, our
    God is merciful.

The Lord preserveth the simple: * I was in misery,
    and he helped me.

Turn again then unto thy rest, O my soul; * for the
    Lord hath rewarded thee.

And why? thou hast delivered my soul from
    death, * mine eyes from tears, and my feet from
    falling.

I will walk before the Lord * in the land of the
    living.

I believed, and therefore will I speak; but I was
   sore troubled: * I said in my haste, All men are
   liars.
What reward shall I give unto the Lord * for all
   the benefits that he hath done unto me?
I will receive the cup of salvation, * and call upon
   the Name of the Lord.
I will pay my vows now in the presence of all his
   people: * right dear in the sight of the Lord is
   the death of his saints.
Behold, O Lord, how that I am thy servant; * I am
   thy servant, and the son of thine handmaid; thou
   hast broken my bonds in sunder.
I will offer to thee the sacrifice of thanksgiving, *
   and will call upon the Name of the Lord.
I will pay my vows unto the Lord, in the sight of
   all his people, * in the courts of the Lord's
   house, even in the midst of thee, O Jerusalem.
   Praise the Lord.

Psalm 117. *Laudate Dominum.*
Alleluia.

O PRAISE the Lord, all ye heathen; * praise him,
   all ye nations.

For his merciful kindness is ever more and more towards us; * and the truth of the Lord endureth for ever. Praise the Lord.

Psalm 118. *Confitemini Domino.*
Alleluia.

O GIVE thanks unto the Lord, for he is gracious; * because his mercy endureth for ever.

Let Israel now confess that he is gracious, * and that his mercy endureth for ever.

Let the house of Aaron now confess, * that his mercy endureth for ever.

Yea, let them now that fear the Lord confess, * that his mercy endureth for ever.

I called upon the Lord in trouble; * and the Lord heard me at large.

The Lord is on my side; * I will not fear what man doeth unto me.

The Lord taketh my part with them that help me; * therefore shall I see my desire upon mine enemies.

It is better to trust in the Lord, * than to put any confidence in man.

It is better to trust in the Lord, * than to put any confidence in princes.

All nations compassed me round about; * but in the Name of the Lord will I destroy them.

They kept me in on every side, they kept me in, I say, on every side; * but in the Name of the Lord will I destroy them.

They came about me like bees, and are extinct even as the fire among the thorns; * for in the Name of the Lord I will destroy them.

Thou hast thrust sore at me, that I might fall; * but the Lord was my help.

The Lord is my strength, and my song; * and is become my salvation.

The voice of joy and health is in the dwellings of the righteous; * the right hand of the Lord bringeth mighty things to pass.

The right hand of the Lord hath the pre-eminence; * the right hand of the Lord bringeth mighty things to pass.

I shall not die, but live, * and declare the works of the Lord.

The Lord hath chastened and corrected me; * but he hath not given me over unto death.

Open me the gates of righteousness, * that I may go into them, and give thanks unto the Lord.

This is the gate of the Lord, * the righteous shall enter into it.

I will thank thee, for thou hast heard me, * and art become my salvation.

The same stone which the builders refused, * is become the head-stone in the corner.

This is the Lord's doing, * and it is marvellous in our eyes.

This is the day which the Lord hath made; * we will rejoice and be glad in it.

Help me now, O Lord: * O Lord, send us now prosperity.

Blessed be he that cometh in the Name of the Lord: * we have wished you good luck, ye that are of the house of the Lord.

God is the Lord who hath shewed us light: * bind the sacrifice with cords, yea, even unto the horns of the altar.

Thou art my God, and I will thank thee; * thou art my God, and I will praise thee.

O give thanks unto the Lord, for he is gracious, * and his mercy endureth for ever.

THE SEVENTEENTH KATHISMA

✠ FIRST STASIS ✠

Psalm 119. *Beati immaculati.*

Alleluia.

BLESSED are those that are undefiled in the way, *
and walk in the law of the Lord.

Blessed are they that keep his testimonies, * and
seek him with their whole heart.

For they who do no wickedness * walk in his
ways.

Thou hast charged * that we shall diligently keep
thy commandments.

O that my ways were made so direct, * that I
might keep thy statutes!

So shall I not be confounded, * while I have
respect unto all thy commandments.

I will thank thee with an unfeigned heart, * when I
shall have learned the judgements of thy
righteousness.

I will keep thy ceremonies; * O forsake me not
utterly.

In quo corriget?

WHEREWITHAL shall a young man cleanse his
way? * even by ruling himself after thy word.

With my whole heart have I sought thee; * O let
me not go wrong out of thy commandments.

Thy words have I hid within my heart, * that I
should not sin against thee.

Blessed art thou, O Lord; * O teach me thy
statutes.

With my lips have I been telling * of all the
judgements of thy mouth.

I have had as great delight in the way of thy
testimonies, * as in all manner of riches.

I will talk of thy commandments, * and have
respect unto thy ways.

My delight shall be in thy statutes, * and I will not
forget thy word.

Retribue servo tuo.

O DO well unto thy servant; * that I may live, and
keep thy word.

Open thou mine eyes; * that I may see the
wondrous things of thy law.

I am a stranger upon earth; * O hide not thy
    commandments from me.
My soul breaketh out for the very fervent desire *
    that it hath alway unto thy judgements.
Thou hast rebuked the proud; * and cursed are
    they that do err from thy commandments.
O turn from me shame and rebuke; * for I have
    kept thy testimonies.
Princes also did sit and speak against me; * but
    thy servant is occupied in thy statutes.
For thy testimonies are my delight, * and my
    counsellors.

Adhæsit pavimento.

My soul cleaveth to the dust; * O quicken thou
    me, according to thy word.
I have acknowledged my ways, and thou heardest
    me: * O teach me thy statutes.
Make me to understand the way of thy
    commandments; * and so shall I talk of thy
    wondrous works.
My soul melteth away for very heaviness; *
    comfort thou me according unto thy word.

Take from me the way of lying, * and cause thou
    me to make much of thy law.
I have chosen the way of truth, * and thy
    judgements have I laid before me.
I have stuck unto thy testimonies; * O Lord,
    confound me not.
I will run the way of thy commandments, * when
    thou hast set my heart at liberty.

Legem pone.

TEACH me, O Lord, the way of thy statutes, * and
    I shall keep it unto the end.
Give me understanding, and I shall keep thy
    law; * yea, I shall keep it with my whole heart.
Make me to go in the path of thy
    commandments; * for therein is my desire.
Incline my heart unto thy testimonies, * and not to
    covetousness.
O turn away mine eyes, lest they behold vanity; *
    and quicken thou me in thy way.
O stablish thy word in thy servant, * that I may
    fear thee.
Take away the rebuke that I am afraid of; * for thy
    judgements are good.

Behold, my delight is in thy commandments; * O
quicken me in thy righteousness.

Et veniat super me.

LET thy loving mercy come also unto me, O Lord,
* even thy salvation, according unto thy word.
So shall I make answer unto my blasphemers; *
for my trust is in thy word.
O take not the word of thy truth utterly out of my
mouth; * for my hope is in thy judgements.
So shall I alway keep thy law; * yea, for ever and
ever.
And I will walk at liberty; * for I seek thy
commandments.
I will speak of thy testimonies also, even before
kings, * and will not be ashamed.
And my delight shall be in thy commandments, *
which I have loved.
My hands also will I lift up unto thy
commandments, which I have loved; * and my
study shall be in thy statutes.

Memor esto servi tui.

O THINK upon thy servant, as concerning thy
  word, * wherein thou hast caused me to put my
  trust.

The same is my comfort in my trouble; * for thy
  word hath quickened me.

The proud have had me exceedingly in derision; *
  yet have I not shrinked from thy law.

For I remembered thine everlasting judgements, O
  Lord, * and received comfort.

I am horribly afraid, * for the ungodly that forsake
  thy law.

Thy statutes have been my songs, * in the house
  of my pilgrimage.

I have thought upon thy Name, O Lord, in the
  night-season, * and have kept thy law.

This I had, * because I kept thy commandments.

Portio mea, Domine.

THOU art my portion, O Lord; * I have promised
  to keep thy law.

I made my humble petition in thy presence with
  my whole heart; * O be merciful unto me,
  according to thy word.

I called mine own ways to remembrance, * and
turned my feet unto thy testimonies.
I made haste, and prolonged not the time, * to
keep thy commandments.
The congregations of the ungodly have robbed
me; * but I have not forgotten thy law.
At midnight I will rise to give thanks unto thee, *
because of thy righteous judgements.
I am a companion of all them that fear thee, * and
keep thy commandments.
The earth, O Lord, is full of thy mercy: * O teach
me thy statutes.

Bonitatem fecisti.

O LORD, thou hast dealt graciously with thy
servant, * according unto thy word.
O learn me true understanding and knowledge; *
for I have believed thy commandments.
Before I was troubled, I went wrong; * but now
have I kept thy word.
Thou art good and gracious; * O teach me thy
statutes.

The proud have imagined a lie against me; * but I will keep thy commandments with my whole heart.

Their heart is as fat as brawn; * but my delight hath been in thy law.

It is good for me that I have been in trouble; * that I may learn thy statutes.

The law of thy mouth is dearer unto me * than thousands of gold and silver.

✠ SECOND STASIS ✠

Manus tuæ fecerunt me.

THY hands have made me and fashioned me: * O give me understanding, that I may learn thy commandments.

They that fear thee will be glad when they see me; * because I have put my trust in thy word.

I know, O Lord, that thy judgements are right, * and that thou of very faithfulness hast caused me to be troubled.

O let thy merciful kindness be my comfort, * according to thy word unto thy servant.

O let thy loving mercies come unto me, that I may live; * for thy law is my delight.

Let the proud be confounded, for they go wickedly about to destroy me; * but I will be occupied in thy commandments.

Let such as fear thee, and have known thy testimonies, * be turned unto me.

O let my heart be sound in thy statutes, * that I be not ashamed.

Defecit anima mea.

MY SOUL hath longed for thy salvation, * and I have a good hope because of thy word.

Mine eyes long sore for thy word; * saying, O when wilt thou comfort me?

For I am become like a bottle in the smoke; * yet do I not forget thy statutes.

How many are the days of thy servant? * when wilt thou be avenged of them that persecute me?

The proud have digged pits for me, * which are not after thy law.

All thy commandments are true: * they persecute me falsely; O be thou my help.

They had almost made an end of me upon earth; *
but I forsook not thy commandments.

O quicken me after thy loving-kindness; * and so
shall I keep the testimonies of thy mouth.

In æternum, Domine.

O LORD, thy word * endureth for ever in heaven.

Thy truth also remaineth from one generation to
another; * thou hast laid the foundation of the
earth, and it abideth.

They continue this day according to thine
ordinance; * for all things serve thee.

If my delight had not been in thy law, * I should
have perished in my trouble.

I will never forget thy commandments; * for with
them thou hast quickened me.

I am thine, O save me, * for I have sought thy
commandments.

The ungodly laid wait for me to destroy me; * but
I will consider thy testimonies.

I see that all things come to an end; * but thy
commandment is exceeding broad.

Quomodo dilexi!

Lord, what love have I unto thy law! * all the day
    long is my study in it.

Thou through thy commandments hast made me
    wiser than mine enemies; * for they are ever
    with me.

I have more understanding than my teachers; * for
    thy testimonies are my study.

I am wiser than the aged; * because I keep thy
    commandments.

I have refrained my feet from every evil way, *
    that I may keep thy word.

I have not shrunk from thy judgements; * for thou
    teachest me.

O how sweet are thy words unto my throat; * yea,
    sweeter than honey unto my mouth.

Through thy commandments I get
    understanding: * therefore I hate all evil ways.

Lucerna pedibus meis.

Thy word is a lantern unto my feet, * and a light
    unto my paths.

I have sworn, and am stedfastly purposed, * to
    keep thy righteous judgements.

I am troubled above measure: * quicken me, O
Lord, according to thy word.

Let the free-will offerings of my mouth please
thee, O Lord; * and teach me thy judgements.

My soul is alway in my hand; * yet do I not forget
thy law.

The ungodly have laid a snare for me; * but yet I
swerved not from thy commandments.

Thy testimonies have I claimed as mine heritage
for ever; * and why? they are the very joy of
my heart.

I have applied my heart to fulfil thy statutes
alway, * even unto the end.

Iniquos odio habui.

I HATE them that imagine evil things; * but thy
law do I love.

Thou art my defence and shield; * and my trust is
in thy word.

Away from me, ye wicked; * I will keep the
commandments of my God.

O stablish me according to thy word, that I may
live; * and let me not be disappointed of my
hope.

Hold thou me up, and I shall be safe; * yea, my
    delight shall be ever in thy statutes.
Thou hast trodden down all them that depart from
    thy statutes; * for they imagine but deceit.
Thou puttest away all the ungodly of the earth like
    dross; * therefore I love thy testimonies.
My flesh trembleth for fear of thee; * and I am
    afraid of thy judgements.

Feci judicium.

I DEAL with the thing that is lawful and right; * O
    give me not over unto mine oppressors.
Make thou thy servant to delight in that which is
    good, * that the proud do me no wrong.
Mine eyes are wasted away with looking for thy
    health, * and for the word of thy righteousness.
O deal with thy servant according unto thy loving
    mercy, * and teach me thy statutes.
I am thy servant, O grant me understanding, * that
    I may know thy testimonies.
It is time for thee, Lord, to lay to thine hand; * for
    they have destroyed thy law.
For I love thy commandments * above gold and
    precious stone.

Therefore hold I straight all thy commandments; *
and all false ways I utterly abhor.

✠ THIRD STASIS ✠

Mirabilia.

THY testimonies are wonderful; * therefore doth
  my soul keep them.
When thy word goeth forth, * it giveth light and
  understanding unto the simple.
I opened my mouth, and drew in my breath; * for
  my delight was in thy commandments.
Look thou upon me, and be merciful unto me, * as
  thou usest to do unto those that love thy Name.
Order my steps in thy word; * and so shall no
  wickedness have dominion over me.
O deliver me from the wrongful dealings of
  men; * and so shall I keep thy commandments.
Shew the light of thy countenance upon thy
  servant, * and teach me thy statutes.
Mine eyes gush out with water, * because men
  keep not thy law.

Justus es, Domine.

RIGHTEOUS art thou, O Lord; * and true is thy
  judgement.
The testimonies that thou hast commanded * are
  exceeding righteous and true.
My zeal hath even consumed me; * because mine
  enemies have forgotten thy words.
Thy word is tried to the uttermost, * and thy
  servant loveth it.
I am small, and of no reputation; * yet do I not
  forget thy commandments.
Thy righteousness is an everlasting
  righteousness, * and thy law is the truth.
Trouble and heaviness have taken hold upon
  me; * yet is my delight in thy commandments.
The righteousness of thy testimonies is
  everlasting: * O grant me understanding, and I
  shall live.

Clamavi in toto corde meo.

I CALL with my whole heart; * hear me, O Lord, I
  will keep thy statutes.
Yea, even unto thee do I call; * help me, and I
  shall keep thy testimonies.

Early in the morning do I cry unto thee; * for in
  thy word is my trust.
Mine eyes prevent the night-watches; * that I
  might be occupied in thy words.
Hear my voice, O Lord, according unto thy
  loving-kindness; * quicken me, according as
  thou art wont.
They draw nigh that of malice persecute me, * and
  are far from thy law.
Be thou nigh at hand, O Lord; * for all thy
  commandments are true.
As concerning thy testimonies, I have known long
  since, * that thou hast grounded them for ever.

Vide humilitatem.

O CONSIDER mine adversity, and deliver me, * for
  I do not forget thy law.
Avenge thou my cause, and deliver me; * quicken
  me, according to thy word.
Health is far from the ungodly; * for they regard
  not thy statutes.
Great is thy mercy, O Lord; * quicken me, as thou
  art wont.

Many there are that trouble me, and persecute me;
* yet do I not swerve from thy testimonies.
It grieveth me when I see the transgressors; *
because they keep not thy law.
Consider, O Lord, how I love thy
commandments; * O quicken me, according to
thy loving-kindness.
Thy word is true from everlasting; * all the
judgements of thy righteousness endure for
evermore.

Principes persecuti sunt.

PRINCES have persecuted me without a cause; *
but my heart standeth in awe of thy word.
I am as glad of thy word, * as one that findeth
great spoils.
As for lies, I hate and abhor them; * but thy law
do I love.
Seven times a day do I praise thee, * because of
thy righteous judgements.
Great is the peace that they have who love thy
law; * and they are not offended at it.
Lord, I have looked for thy saving health, * and
done after thy commandments.

My soul hath kept thy testimonies, * and loved
them exceedingly.
I have kept thy commandments and testimonies; *
for all my ways are before thee.

Appropinquet deprecatio.

LET my complaint come before thee, O Lord; *
give me understanding, according to thy word.
Let my supplication come before thee; * deliver
me, according to thy word.
My lips shall speak of thy praise, * when thou hast
taught me thy statutes.
Yea, my tongue shall sing of thy word; * for all
thy commandments are righteous.
Let thine hand help me; * for I have chosen thy
commandments.
I have longed for thy saving health, O Lord; * and
in thy law is my delight.
O let my soul live, and it shall praise thee; * and
thy judgements shall help me.
I have gone astray like a sheep that is lost; * O
seek thy servant, for I do not forget thy
commandments.

THE EIGHTEENTH KATHISMA

✠ FIRST STASIS ✠

Psalm 120. *Ad Dominum.*
A song of ascents.

WHEN I was in trouble I called upon the Lord, *
and he heard me.

Deliver my soul, O Lord, from lying lips, * and
from a deceitful tongue.

What reward shall be given or done unto thee,
thou false tongue? * even mighty and sharp
arrows, with hot burning coals.

Woe is me, that I am constrained to dwell with
Mesech, * and to have my habitation among the
tents of Kedar.

My soul hath long dwelt among them * that are
enemies unto peace.

I labour for peace; but when I speak unto them
thereof, * they make them ready to battle.

Psalm 121. *Levavi oculus.*

A song of ascents.

I WILL lift up mine eyes unto the hills, * from whence cometh my help.

My help cometh even from the Lord, * who hath made heaven and earth.

He will not suffer thy foot to be moved; * and he that keepeth thee will not sleep.

Behold, he that keepeth Israel * shall neither slumber nor sleep.

The Lord himself is thy keeper; * the Lord is thy defence upon thy right hand;

So that the sun shall not burn thee by day, * neither the moon by night.

The Lord shall preserve thee from all evil; * yea, it is even he that shall keep thy soul.

The Lord shall preserve thy going out, and thy coming in, * from this time forth for evermore.

Psalm 122. *Lætatus sum.*

A song of ascents.

I WAS glad when they said unto me, * We will go
    into the house of the Lord.

Our feet shall stand in thy gates, * O Jerusalem.

Jerusalem is built as a city * that is at unity in
    itself.

For thither the tribes go up, even the tribes of the
    Lord, * to testify unto Israel, to give thanks
    unto the Name of the Lord.

For there is the seat of judgement, * even the seat
    of the house of David.

O pray for the peace of Jerusalem; * they shall
    prosper that love thee.

Peace be within thy walls, * and plenteousness
    within thy palaces.

For my brethren and companions' sakes, * I will
    wish thee prosperity.

Yea, because of the house of the Lord our God, * I
    will seek to do thee good.

Psalm 123. *Ad te levavi oculos meos.*

A song of ascents.

UNTO thee lift I up mine eyes, * O thou that dwellest in the heavens.

Behold, even as the eyes of servants look unto the hand of their masters, and as the eyes of a maiden unto the hand of her mistress, * even so our eyes wait upon the Lord our God, until he have mercy upon us.

Have mercy upon us, O Lord, have mercy upon us; * for we are utterly despised.

Our soul is filled with the scornful reproof of the wealthy, * and with the despitefulness of the proud.

Psalm 124. *Nisi quia Dominus.*

A song of ascents.

IF THE Lord himself had not been on our side,
now may Israel say; * if the Lord himself had
not been on our side, when men rose up against
us;

They had swallowed us up quick; * when they
were so wrathfully displeased at us.

Yea, the waters had drowned us, * and the stream
had gone over our soul.

The deep waters of the proud * had gone even
over our soul.

But praised be the Lord, * who hath not given us
over for a prey unto their teeth.

Our soul is escaped even as a bird out of the snare
of the fowler; * the snare is broken, and we are
delivered.

Our help standeth in the Name of the Lord, * who
hath made heaven and earth.

Psalm 125. *Qui confidunt.*
A song of ascents.

THEY that put their trust in the Lord shall be even
as the mount Sion, * which may not be
removed, but standeth fast for ever.

The hills stand about Jerusalem; * even so
standeth the Lord round about his people, from
this time forth for evermore.

For the rod of the ungodly cometh not into the lot
of the righteous; * lest the righteous put their
hand unto wickedness.

Do well, O Lord, * unto those that are good and
true of heart.

As for such as turn back unto their own
wickedness, * the Lord shall lead them forth
with the evil-doers; but peace shall be upon
Israel.

Psalm 126. *In convertendo.*
A song of ascents.

WHEN the Lord turned again the captivity of
Sion, * then were we like unto them that dream.

Then was our mouth filled with laughter, * and
our tongue with joy.
Then said they among the heathen, * The Lord
hath done great things for them.
Yea, the Lord hath done great things for us
already; * whereof we rejoice.
Turn our captivity, O Lord, * as the rivers in the
south.
They that sow in tears * shall reap in joy.
He that now goeth on his way weeping, and
beareth forth good seed, * shall doubtless come
again with joy, and bring his sheaves with him.

Psalm 127. *Nisi Dominus.*
A song of ascents.

EXCEPT the Lord build the house, * their labour is
but lost that build it.
Except the Lord keep the city, * the watchman
waketh but in vain.
It is but lost labour that ye haste to rise up early,
and so late take rest, and eat the bread of
carefulness; * for so he giveth his beloved
sleep.

Lo, children and the fruit of the womb, * are an
    heritage and gift that cometh of the Lord.
Like as the arrows in the hand of the giant, * even
    so are the young children.
Happy is the man that hath his quiver full of
    them; * they shall not be ashamed when they
    speak with their enemies in the gate.

Psalm 128. *Beati omnes.*

A song of ascents.

BLESSED are all they that fear the Lord, * and
    walk in his ways.
For thou shalt eat the labours of thine hands: * O
    well is thee, and happy shalt thou be.
Thy wife shall be as the fruitful vine * upon the
    walls of thine house.
Thy children like the olive-branches * round about
    thy table.
Lo, thus shall the man be blessed * that feareth the
    Lord.
The Lord from out of Sion shall so bless thee, *
    that thou shalt see Jerusalem in prosperity all
    thy life long.

Yea, that thou shalt see thy children's children, *
and peace upon Israel.

Psalm 129. *Sæpe expugnaverunt.*
A song of ascents.

MANY a time have they fought against me from
my youth up, * may Israel now say.

Yea, many a time have they vexed me from my
youth up; * but they have not prevailed against
me.

The plowers plowed upon my back, * and made
long furrows.

But the righteous Lord * hath hewn the snares of
the ungodly in pieces.

Let them be confounded and turned backward, *
as many as have evil will at Sion.

Let them be even as the grass growing upon the
house-tops, * which withereth afore it be
plucked up;

Whereof the mower filleth not his hand, * neither
he that bindeth up the sheaves his bosom.

So that they who go by say not so much as, The
Lord prosper you; * we wish you good luck in
the Name of the Lord.

✠ THIRD STASIS ✠

Psalm 130. *De profundis.*
A song of ascents.

OUT of the deep have I called unto thee, O Lord; *
Lord, hear my voice.

O let thine ears consider well * the voice of my
complaint.

If thou, Lord, wilt be extreme to mark what is
done amiss, * O Lord, who may abide it?

For there is mercy with thee; * therefore shalt thou
be feared.

I look for the Lord; my soul doth wait for him; *
in his word is my trust.

My soul fleeth unto the Lord * before the morning
watch, I say, before the morning watch.

O Israel, trust in the Lord, for with the Lord there
is mercy, * and with him is plenteous
redemption.

And he shall redeem Israel * from all his sins.

Psalm 131. *Domine, non est.*

A song of ascents.

LORD, I am not high-minded; * I have no proud
looks.

I do not exercise myself in great matters * which
are too high for me.

But I refrain my soul, and keep it low, like as a
child that is weaned from his mother: * yea, my
soul is even as a weaned child.

O Israel, trust in the Lord * from this time forth
for evermore.

Psalm 132. *Memento, Domine.*

A song of ascents.

LORD, remember David, * and all his trouble;

How he sware unto the Lord, * and vowed a vow
unto the Almighty God of Jacob;

I will not come within the tabernacle of mine
house, * nor climb up into my bed;

I will not suffer mine eyes to sleep, nor mine eye-
lids to slumber; * neither the temples of my
head to take any rest;

Until I find out a place for the temple of the
Lord; * an habitation for the mighty God of
Jacob.
Lo, we heard of the same at Ephrata, * and found
it in the wood.
We will go into his tabernacle, * and fall low on
our knees before his footstool.
Arise, O Lord, into thy resting-place; * thou, and
the ark of thy strength.
Let thy priests be clothed with righteousness; *
and let thy saints sing with joyfulness.
For thy servant David's sake, * turn not away the
presence of thine Anointed.
The Lord hath made a faithful oath unto David, *
and he shall not shrink from it;
Of the fruit of thy body * shall I set upon thy seat.
If thy children will keep my covenant, and my
testimonies that I shall learn them; * their
children also shall sit upon thy seat for
evermore.
For the Lord hath chosen Sion to be an habitation
for himself; * he hath longed for her.
This shall be my rest for ever: * here will I dwell,
for I have a delight therein.

I will bless her victuals with increase, * and will
satisfy her poor with bread.
I will deck her priests with health, * and her saints
shall rejoice and sing.
There shall I make the horn of David to flourish: *
I have ordained a lantern for mine Anointed.
As for his enemies, I shall clothe them with
shame; * but upon himself shall his crown
flourish.

Psalm 133. *Ecce, quam bonum!*
A song of ascents.

BEHOLD, how good and joyful a thing it is, *
brethren, to dwell together in unity!
It is like the precious ointment upon the head, that
ran down unto the beard, * even unto Aaron's
beard, and went down to the skirts of his
clothing.
Like as the dew of Hermon, * which fell upon the
hill of Sion.
For there the Lord promised his blessing, * and
life for evermore.

Psalm 134. *Ecce nunc.*

A song of ascents.

BEHOLD now, praise the Lord, * all ye servants of
    the Lord;

Ye that by night stand in the house of the Lord, *
    even in the courts of the house of our God.

Lift up your hands in the sanctuary, * and praise
    the Lord.

The Lord that made heaven and earth * give thee
    blessing out of Sion.

THE NINETEENTH KATHISMA

✠ FIRST STASIS ✠

Psalm 135. *Laudate Nomen.*

Alleluia.

O PRAISE the Lord, laud ye the Name of the
Lord; * praise it, O ye servants of the Lord;
Ye that stand in the house of the Lord, * in the
courts of the house of our God.
O praise the Lord, for the Lord is gracious; * O
sing praises unto his Name, for it is lovely.
For why? the Lord hath chosen Jacob unto
himself, * and Israel for his own possession.
For I know that the Lord is great, * and that our
Lord is above all gods.
Whatsoever the Lord pleased, that did he in
heaven and in earth; * and in the sea, and in all
deep places.
He bringeth forth the clouds from the ends of the
world, * and sendeth forth lightnings with the
rain, bringing the winds out of his treasures.

He smote the first-born of Egypt, * both of man and beast.

He hath sent tokens and wonders into the midst of thee, O thou land of Egypt, * upon Pharaoh, and all his servants.

He smote divers nations, * and slew mighty kings;

Sehon king of the Amorites, and Og the king of Basan; * and all the kingdoms of Canaan;

And gave their land to be an heritage, * even an heritage unto Israel his people.

Thy Name, O Lord, endureth for ever; * so doth thy memorial, O Lord, from one generation to another.

For the Lord will avenge his people, * and be gracious unto his servants.

As for the images of the heathen, they are but silver and gold; * the work of men's hands.

They have mouths, and speak not; * eyes have they, but they see not.

They have ears, and yet they hear not; * neither is there any breath in their mouths.

They that make them are like unto them; * and so are all they that put their trust in them.

Praise the Lord, ye house of Israel; * praise the
Lord, ye house of Aaron.

Praise the Lord, ye house of Levi; * ye that fear
the Lord, praise the Lord.

Praised be the Lord out of Sion, * who dwelleth at
Jerusalem.

Psalm 136. *Confitemini.*
Alleluia.

O GIVE thanks unto the Lord, for he is gracious: *
and his mercy endureth for ever.

O give thanks unto the God of all gods: * for his
mercy endureth for ever.

O thank the Lord of all lords: * for his mercy
endureth for ever.

Who only doeth great wonders: * for his mercy
endureth for ever.

Who by his excellent wisdom made the heavens: *
for his mercy endureth for ever.

Who laid out the earth above the waters: * for his
mercy endureth for ever.

Who hath made great lights: * for his mercy
endureth for ever;

The sun to rule the day: * for his mercy endureth
for ever;
The moon and the stars to govern the night: * for
his mercy endureth for ever.
Who smote Egypt with their first-born: * for his
mercy endureth for ever;
And brought out Israel from among them: * for
his mercy endureth for ever;
With a mighty hand, and stretched out arm: * for
his mercy endureth for ever.
Who divided the Red sea in two parts: * for his
mercy endureth for ever;
And made Israel to go through the midst of it: *
for his mercy endureth for ever.
But as for Pharaoh and his host, he overthrew
them in the Red sea: * for his mercy endureth
for ever.
Who led his people through the wilderness: * for
his mercy endureth for ever.
Who smote great kings: * for his mercy endureth
for ever;
Yea, and slew mighty kings: * for his mercy
endureth for ever;

Sehon king of the Amorites: * for his mercy
   endureth for ever;
And Og the king of Basan: * for his mercy
   endureth for ever;
And gave away their land for an heritage: * for his
   mercy endureth for ever;
Even for an heritage unto Israel his servant: * for
   his mercy endureth for ever.
Who remembered us when we were in trouble: *
   for his mercy endureth for ever;
And hath delivered us from our enemies: * for his
   mercy endureth for ever.
Who giveth food to all flesh: * for his mercy
   endureth for ever.
O give thanks unto the God of heaven: * for his
   mercy endureth for ever.
O give thanks unto the Lord of lords: * for his
   mercy endureth for ever.

Psalm 137. *Super flumina.*
For David. A psalm of Jeremias.
BY THE waters of Babylon we sat down and
   wept, * when we remembered thee, O Sion.

As for our harps, we hanged them up * upon the trees that are therein.

For they that led us away captive required of us then a song, and melody in our heaviness: * Sing us one of the songs of Sion.

How shall we sing the Lord's song * in a strange land?

If I forget thee, O Jerusalem, * let my right hand forget her cunning.

If I do not remember thee, let my tongue cleave to the roof of my mouth; * yea, if I prefer not Jerusalem in my mirth.

Remember the children of Edom, O Lord, in the day of Jerusalem; * how they said, Down with it, down with it, even to the ground.

O daughter of Babylon, wasted with misery; * yea, happy shall he be that rewardeth thee, as thou hast served us.

Blessed shall he be that taketh thy children, * and throweth them against the stones.

Psalm 138. *Confitebor tibi.*

A psalm of David, of Aggæus and Zacharias.

I WILL give thanks unto thee, O Lord, with my whole heart; * even before the gods will I sing praise unto thee.

I will worship toward thy holy temple, and praise thy Name, because of thy loving-kindness and truth; * for thou hast magnified thy Name and thy word above all things.

When I called upon thee, thou heardest me; * and enduedst my soul with much strength.

All the kings of the earth shall praise thee, O Lord; * for they have heard the words of thy mouth.

Yea, they shall sing in the ways of the Lord, * that great is the glory of the Lord.

For though the Lord be high, yet hath he respect unto the lowly; * as for the proud, he beholdeth them afar off.

Though I walk in the midst of trouble, yet shalt thou refresh me; * thou shalt stretch forth thy hand upon the furiousness of mine enemies, and thy right hand shall save me.

The Lord shall make good his loving-kindness toward me; * yea, thy mercy, O Lord, endureth for ever; despise not then the works of thine own hands.

Psalm 139. *Domine, probasti.*
For the end. A psalm of David.

O LORD, thou hast searched me out and known me; * thou knowest my down-sitting and mine up-rising, thou understandest my thoughts long before.

Thou art about my path, and about my bed; * and spiest out all my ways.

For lo, there is not a word in my tongue, * but thou, O Lord, knowest it altogether.

Thou hast fashioned me behind and before, * and laid thine hand upon me.

Such knowledge is too wonderful and excellent for me; * I cannot attain unto it.

Whither shall I go then from thy Spirit? * or whither shall I go then from thy presence?

If I climb up into heaven, thou art there; * if I go
down to hell, thou art there also.
If I take the wings of the morning, * and remain in
the uttermost parts of the sea;
Even there also shall thy hand lead me, * and thy
right hand shall hold me.
If I say, Peradventure the darkness shall cover
me; * then shall my night be turned to day.
Yea, the darkness is no darkness with thee, but the
night is as clear as the day; * the darkness and
light to thee are both alike.
For my reins are thine; * thou hast covered me in
my mother's womb.
I will give thanks unto thee, for I am fearfully and
wonderfully made: * marvellous are thy works,
and that my soul knoweth right well.
My bones are not hid from thee, * though I be
made secretly, and fashioned beneath in the
earth.
Thine eyes did see my substance, yet being
unperfect; * and in thy book were all my
members written;
Which day by day were fashioned, * when as yet
there was none of them.

How dear are thy counsels unto me, O God; * O
how great is the sum of them!

If I tell them, they are more in number than the
sand: * when I wake up I am present with thee.

Wilt thou not slay the wicked, O God? * depart
from me, ye blood-thirsty men.

For they speak unrighteously against thee; * and
thine enemies take thy Name in vain.

Do not I hate them, O Lord, that hate thee? * and
am not I grieved with those that rise up against
thee?

Yea, I hate them right sore; * even as though they
were mine enemies.

Try me, O God, and seek the ground of my
heart; * prove me, and examine my thoughts.

Look well if there be any way of wickedness in
me: * and lead me in the way everlasting.

Psalm 140. *Eripe me, Domine.*
For the end. A psalm of David.

DELIVER me, O Lord, from the evil man; * and
preserve me from the wicked man.

Who imagine mischief in their hearts, * and stir
up strife all the day long.

They have sharpened their tongues like a
  serpent; * adders' poison is under their lips.
Keep me, O Lord, from the hands of the
  ungodly; * preserve me from the wicked men,
  who are purposed to overthrow my goings.
The proud have laid a snare for me, and spread a
  net abroad with cords; * yea, and set traps in
  my way.
I said unto the Lord, Thou art my God, * hear the
  voice of my prayers, O Lord.
O Lord God, thou strength of my health; * thou
  hast covered my head in the day of the battle.
Let not the ungodly have his desire, O Lord; * let
  not his mischievous imagination prosper, lest
  they be too proud.
Let the mischief of their own lips fall upon the
  head of them * that compass me about.
Let hot burning coals fall upon them; * let them
  be cast into the fire and into the pit, that they
  never rise up again.
A man full of words shall not prosper upon the
  earth: * evil shall hunt the wicked person to
  overthrow him.

Sure I am that the Lord will avenge the poor, * and maintain the cause of the helpless.

The righteous also shall give thanks unto thy Name; * and the just shall continue in thy sight.

✠ THIRD STASIS ✠

Psalm 141. *Domine, clamavi.*
A psalm of David.

LORD, I call upon thee, haste thee unto me! * and consider my voice when I cry unto thee.

Let my prayer be set forth in thy sight as the incense; * and let the lifting up of my hands be an evening sacrifice.

Set a watch, O Lord, before my mouth, * and keep the door of my lips.

O let not mine heart be inclined to any evil thing; * let me not be occupied in ungodly works with the men that work wickedness, lest I eat of such things as please them.

Let the righteous rather smite me friendly, * and reprove me.

But let not their precious balms break my head; * yea, I will pray yet against their wickedness.

Let their judges be overthrown in stony places, *
that they may hear my words, for they are
sweet.

Our bones lie scattered before the pit, * like as
when one breaketh and heweth wood upon the
earth.

But mine eyes look unto thee, O Lord God; * in
thee is my trust, O cast not out my soul.

Keep me from the snare that they have laid for
me, * and from the traps of the wicked doers.

Let the ungodly fall into their own nets together, *
and let me ever escape them.

Psalm 142. *Voce mea ad Dominum.*

*A psalm of instruction for David. When he was in
the cave; a prayer.*

I CRIED unto the Lord with my voice; * yea, even
unto the Lord did I make my supplication.

I poured out my complaints before him, * and
shewed him of my trouble.

When my spirit was in heaviness thou knewest my
path; * in the way wherein I walked have they
privily laid a snare for me.

I looked also upon my right hand, * and saw there was no man that would know me.

I had no place to flee unto, * and no man cared for my soul.

I cried unto thee, O Lord, and said, * Thou art my hope, and my portion in the land of the living.

Consider my complaint; * for I am brought very low.

O deliver me from my persecutors; * for they are too strong for me.

Bring my soul out of prison, that I may give thanks unto thy Name; * which thing if thou wilt grant me, then shall the righteous resort unto my company.

Psalm 143. *Domine, exaudi.*

A psalm of David when his son pursued him.

HEAR my prayer, O Lord, and consider my
desire; * hearken unto me for thy truth and
righteousness' sake.

And enter not into judgement with thy servant; *
for in thy sight shall no man living be justified.

For the enemy hath persecuted my soul; he hath
smitten my life down to the ground; * he hath
laid me in the darkness, as the men that have
been long dead.

Therefore is my spirit vexed within me, * and my
heart within me is desolate.

Yet do I remember the time past; I muse upon all
thy works; * yea, I exercise myself in the works
of thy hands.

I stretch forth my hands unto thee; * my soul
gaspeth unto thee as a thirsty land.

Hear me, O Lord, and that soon, for my spirit
waxeth faint; * hide not thy face from me, lest I
be like unto them that go down into the pit.

O let me hear thy loving-kindness betimes in the
morning, for in thee is my trust: * shew thou me

the way that I should walk in, for I lift up my
soul unto thee.

Deliver me, O Lord, from mine enemies; * for I
flee unto thee to hide me.

Teach me to do the thing that pleaseth thee, for
thou art my God: * let thy loving Spirit lead me
forth into the land of righteousness.

Quicken me, O Lord, for thy Name's sake; * and
for thy righteousness' sake bring my soul out of
trouble.

And of thy goodness slay mine enemies, * and
destroy all them that vex my soul; for I am thy
servant.

THE TWENTIETH KATHISMA

✠ FIRST STASIS ✠

Psalm 144. *Benedictus Dominus.*
A psalm of David concerning Goliath.

BLESSED be the Lord my strength, * who teacheth
 my hands to war, and my fingers to fight;

My hope and my fortress, my castle and deliverer,
 my defender in whom I trust; * who subdueth
 my people that is under me.

Lord, what is man, that thou hast such respect
 unto him? * or the son of man, that thou so
 regardest him?

Man is like a thing of nought; * his time passeth
 away like a shadow.

Bow thy heavens, O Lord, and come down; *
 touch the mountains, and they shall smoke.

Cast forth thy lightning, and tear them; * shoot out
 thine arrows, and consume them.

Send down thine hand from above; * deliver me,
 and take me out of the great waters, from the
 hand of strange children;

Whose mouth talketh of vanity, * and their right
hand is a right hand of wickedness.

I will sing a new song unto thee, O God; * and
sing praises unto thee upon a ten-stringed lute.

Thou hast given victory unto kings, * and hast
delivered David thy servant from the peril of
the sword.

Save me, and deliver me from the hand of strange
children, * whose mouth talketh of vanity, and
their right hand is a right hand of iniquity.

That our sons may grow up as the young plants, *
and that our daughters may be as the polished
corners of the temple.

That our garners may be full and plenteous with
all manner of store; * that our sheep may bring
forth thousands and ten thousands in our streets.

That our oxen may be strong to labour, that there
be no decay, * no leading into captivity, and no
complaining in our streets.

Happy are the people that are in such a case; *
yea, blessed are the people who have the Lord
for their God.

Psalm 145. *Exaltabo te, Deus.*

A psalm of praise of David.

I WILL magnify thee, O God, my King; * and I
    will praise thy Name for ever and ever.

Every day will I give thanks unto thee; * and
    praise thy Name for ever and ever.

Great is the Lord, and marvellous worthy to be
    praised; * there is no end of his greatness.

One generation shall praise thy works unto
    another, * and declare thy power.

As for me, I will be talking of thy worship, * thy
    glory, thy praise, and wondrous works;

So that men shall speak of the might of thy
    marvellous acts; * and I will also tell of thy
    greatness.

The memorial of thine abundant kindness shall be
    shewed; * and men shall sing of thy
    righteousness.

The Lord is gracious and merciful; * long-
    suffering and of great goodness.

The Lord is loving unto every man; * and his
    mercy is over all his works.

All thy works praise thee, O Lord; * and thy saints
    give thanks unto thee.

They shew the glory of thy kingdom, * and talk of
thy power;

That thy power, thy glory, and mightiness of thy
kingdom, * might be known unto men.

Thy kingdom is an everlasting kingdom, * and thy
dominion endureth throughout all ages.

The Lord upholdeth all such as fall, * and lifteth
up all those that are down.

The eyes of all wait upon thee, O Lord; * and thou
givest them their meat in due season.

Thou openest thine hand, * and fillest all things
living with plenteousness.

The Lord is righteous in all his ways, * and holy
in all his works.

The Lord is nigh unto all them that call upon
him; * yea, all such as call upon him faithfully.

He will fulfil the desire of them that fear him; * he
also will hear their cry, and will help them.

The Lord preserveth all them that love him; * but
scattereth abroad all the ungodly.

My mouth shall speak the praise of the Lord; *
and let all flesh give thanks unto his holy Name
for ever and ever.

Psalm 146. *Lauda, anima mea.*

Alleluia. A psalm of Aggæus and Zacharias.

PRAISE the Lord, O my soul; while I live will I
praise the Lord; * yea, as long as I have any
being, I will sing praises unto my God.

O put not your trust in princes, nor in any child of
man; * for there is no help in them.

For when the breath of man goeth forth he shall
turn again to his earth, * and then all his
thoughts perish.

Blessed is he that hath the God of Jacob for his
help, * and whose hope is in the Lord his God;

Who made heaven and earth, the sea, and all that
therein is; * who keepeth his promise for ever;

Who helpeth them to right that suffer wrong; *
who feedeth the hungry.

The Lord looseth men out of prison; * the Lord
giveth sight to the blind.

The Lord helpeth them that are fallen; * the Lord
careth for the righteous.

The Lord careth for the strangers, he defendeth the
  fatherless and widow: * as for the way of the
  ungodly, he turneth it upside down.
The Lord thy God, O Sion, shall be King for
  evermore, * and throughout all generations.

Psalm 147. *Laudate Dominum.*

Alleluia. A psalm of Aggæus and Zacharias.

O PRAISE the Lord, for it is a good thing to sing
  praises unto our God; * yea, a joyful and
  pleasant thing it is to be thankful.
The Lord doth build up Jerusalem, * and gather
  together the out-casts of Israel.
He healeth those that are broken in heart, * and
  giveth medicine to heal their sickness.
He telleth the number of the stars, * and calleth
  them all by their names.
Great is our Lord, and great is his power; * yea,
  and his wisdom is infinite.
The Lord setteth up the meek; * and bringeth the
  ungodly down to the ground.
O sing unto the Lord with thanksgiving; * sing
  praises upon the harp unto our God;

Who covereth the heaven with clouds, and
   prepareth rain for the earth; * and maketh the
   grass to grow upon the mountains, and herb for
   the use of men;
Who giveth fodder unto the cattle, * and feedeth
   the young ravens that call upon him.
He hath no pleasure in the strength of an horse; *
   neither delighteth he in any man's legs.
But the Lord's delight is in them that fear him, *
   and put their trust in his mercy.
Praise the Lord, O Jerusalem; * praise thy God, O
   Sion.
For he hath made fast the bars of thy gates, * and
   hath blessed thy children within thee.
He maketh peace in thy borders, * and filleth thee
   with the flour of wheat.
He sendeth forth his commandment upon earth, *
   and his word runneth very swiftly.
He giveth snow like wool, * and scattereth the
   hoar-frost like ashes.
He casteth forth his ice like morsels: * who is able
   to abide his frost?
He sendeth out his word, and melteth them: * he
   bloweth with his wind, and the waters flow.

He sheweth his word unto Jacob, * his statutes
and ordinances unto Israel.
He hath not dealt so with any nation; * neither
have the heathen knowledge of his laws.

✠ THIRD STASIS ✠

Psalm 148. *Laudate Dominum.*

Alleluia. A psalm of Aggæus and Zacharias.

O PRAISE the Lord of heaven: * praise him in the
height.
Praise him, all ye angels of his: * praise him, all
his host.
Praise him, sun and moon: * praise him, all ye
stars and light.
Praise him, all ye heavens, * and ye waters that
are above the heavens.
Let them praise the Name of the Lord: * for he
spake the word, and they were made; he
commanded, and they were created.
He hath made them fast for ever and ever: * he
hath given them a law which shall not be
broken.

Praise the Lord upon earth, * ye dragons, and all deeps;

Fire and hail, snow and vapours, * wind and storm, fulfilling his word;

Mountains and all hills; * fruitful trees and all cedars;

Beasts and all cattle; * worms and feathered fowls;

Kings of the earth and all people; * princes and all judges of the world;

Young men and maidens, old men and children, praise the Name of the Lord: * for his Name only is excellent, and his praise above heaven and earth.

He shall exalt the horn of his people; all his saints shall praise him; * even the children of Israel, even the people that serveth him.

Psalm 149. *Cantate Domino.*

Alleluia.

O SING unto the Lord a new song; * let the
    congregation of saints praise him.

Let Israel rejoice in him that made him, * and let
    the children of Sion be joyful in their King.

Let them praise his Name in the dance: * let them
    sing praises unto him with tabret and harp.

For the Lord hath pleasure in his people, * and
    helpeth the meek-hearted.

Let the saints be joyful with glory; * let them
    rejoice in their beds.

Let the praises of God be in their mouth; * and a
    two-edged sword in their hands;

To be avenged of the heathen, * and to rebuke the
    people;

To bind their kings in chains, * and their nobles
    with links of iron.

That they may be avenged of them, as it is
    written, * Such honour have all his saints.

Psalm 150. *Laudate Dominum.*
Alleluia.

O PRAISE God in his holiness: * praise him in the firmament of his power.

Praise him in his noble acts: * praise him according to his excellent greatness.

Praise him in the sound of the trumpet: * praise him upon the lute and harp.

Praise him in the cymbals and dances: * praise him upon the strings and pipe.

Praise him upon the well-tuned cymbals: * praise him upon the loud cymbals.

Let every thing that hath breath * praise the Lord.

Psalm 151. *Eram inter fratres.*

This psalm is ascribed to David, and is outside the number. When he slew Goliath in single combat.

LITTLE was I among my brethren; * a younger brother in my father's house.

My hands, they made an instrument of musick; * my fingers, a psaltery they prepared.

And who shall bring back tidings to my master? * The Lord himself, himself gives ear.

Himself sent forth his messenger, * and took me from among the sheep of my father; and with the oil of his anointing he anointed me.

Comely my brethren were, and tall, * and yet they found not favor with the Lord.

But I, I sallied forth to meet the Philistine; * and he reviled me by all his idols.

But I drew forth the sword that was beside him: * I cut off his head with it, and from the sons of Israel removed reproach.

ACKNOWLEDGMENTS

A DEBT of gratitude is owed to the anonymous priest who, having translated the Greek subtitles, graciously permitted their use with this psalter; to Monk Joseph of eternal memory for his translation of Psalm 151; and to those who, both wittingly and unwittingly, have aided the success of this project by their criticism and encouragement.

COPYRIGHT